Good Housekeeping
Consumer Guide

Your
Home &
the Law

Good Housekeeping
Consumer Guide

Your Home & the Law

Justin Gray

EBURY PRESS · LONDON

First published in 1995

1 3 5 7 9 10 8 6 4 2

First published in the United Kingdom in 1995 by
Ebury Press · Random House · 20 Vauxhall Bridge Road · London SW1V 2SA

Random House Australia (Pty) Limited
20 Alfred Street · Milsons Point · Sydney · New South Wales 2061 · Australia

Random House New Zealand Limited
18 Poland Road · Glenfield
Auckland 10 · New Zealand

Random House South Africa (Pty) Limited
PO Box 337 · Bergvlei · South Africa

Random House UK Limited Reg. No. 954009

A CIP catalogue record for this book is available from the British Library.

Editor: Alison Wormleighton
Design: Martin Lovelock

ISBN: 0 09 180693 3

Printed and bound in Great Britain by Clays Limited, St Ives, plc.

Contents

Introduction

An Englishman's home is his castle, so the saying goes. But what rights do you have regarding your property, and what can you do about neighbours and other people who threaten to interfere with the privacy and comfort your home offers? The law does not afford absolute protection, and the State and your local council retain considerable powers over what you can do with your property. More specific rights, obligations and restrictions can develop between you and your neighbours, such as someone having a right of way over your drive to get to their house. These rights are not the concern of the state or your council, so that it is up to you to enforce them yourself, either by negotiation or in court, in the same way that you might enforce a contract between you.

This book is a guide to what you can and can't do regarding matters that arise in relation to your home, whether you are the owner or a tenant. It outlines some of the principles that should be applied in certain circumstances, so that you can know your rights and obligations.

For the more serious one-off occurrences like a Compulsory Purchase Order on your home, or extensive damage to it, it would be better to refer to a solicitor; here we are dealing with everyday problems such as trespass and lesser damage.

THE LAST RESORT

A constant message throughout this book is that you should not go to court except in serious circumstances, where an agreement or compromise appears to be impossible. You can use this book to get an idea of what your rights are so that you are in a better position to come to a compromise (*see* Chapter 7 for quick and easy methods of getting orders from the court). This book is not intended as something you can use to issue a flurry of writs against obnoxious neighbours. The law is normally clear on the principles that should be applied, but the courts are reluctant to see every problem that may arise end up in litigation.

Litigation can be extremely expensive and the process can also be frustrating and protracted and cause further arguments afterwards. Court proceedings are a forum of last resort for settling disputes, as they are adversarial and disconcerting to anyone involved – barristers often ask questions in cross-examination that nobody, not even the person they are representing, would ever consider asking normally.

The law exists so you can preserve your rights and you must be allowed to exercise those rights when they appear to be being violated. If you understand the nature of your rights, you will feel more comfortable in maintaining what you are entitled to by the use of the courts, or seeking the advice of a solicitor. The law exists not to be used as a stick to beat someone with, but to ensure that a fair balance is struck between the parties.

Remember Many of the issues that will be outlined are complicated, and you should use a solicitor when the matter is not clear-cut, and cannot be resolved between yourselves.

THE NATURE OF THE LAW

The law relating to the home goes back to the earliest traces of our legal history when people had very different values from today, so you may find that the law in some areas is rather archaic, and places too much emphasis on having actual title to the property. The law has over the centuries been adapted though, and one of the main reasons it has not been fully updated is that few people actually go to court.

Much of the law we will come across is common law. If the law is unclear on an issue, then the matter goes to court and the judge applies the fairest decision, taking into account the other principles of law that relate to it. This decision may be followed in similar situations later. Home ownership is such an ancient area of law, that most of the associated problems have developed legal solutions.

Remember the law may change in the future, particularly in relation to planning and building regulations (*see* chapter 6).

There are some differences between the law in Scotland and the law in England and Wales, but the broad principles are the same. We will cover the variations as they occur.

Rights in relation to other people

The law regulates the way people come into contact with each other, significantly through criminal law, generally where the interference with another person's life is deliberate or intentional. It also imposes another regulation, known as 'tort law' or 'obligations', which concerns the obligations that people should have for others in situations where no malice or prospect of personal gain is involved. Tort law does not normally involve making people do particular things; it makes sure they do not do certain things which might interfere with other people.

Rights over your property

The same principles as above apply to the regulations about people interfering with someone else's property. While many acts are so severe that they can constitute a crime against your property, there are other situations where no harm is intended yet certain restrictions still apply. This ensures that property is respected.

Specific rights

In relation to property which is land
• Particular rights can attach to the property you buy if the property includes land.

Example Mr A and Mr B living next door to each other might come to an agreement that neither of them build a wall at the front of their adjoining properties, as the view might be spoiled. This is all very well for Mr A and Mr B while they are still living there, but the agreement is not much use when one of them moves house and Mr C moves in. However, sometimes this sort of agreement can attach to the property as well as to

Mr A and Mr B, so that the rights and obligations under it are inherited by anyone else who buys the property from them. The title deeds to your own property may well include a clause such as this example.

- The right to do something on your neighbour's property may develop with the land.

Example If your neighbour's path has always been used as a shortcut to your own house, whether by you or by previous owners, then this may eventually develop into a specific right of whoever owns your property to use that path for these purposes. This can also apply to any development or demolition your neighbour might do to his property. It may affect the light coming to your property, or maybe the structure of your building depends on the existing structure of the buildings on his property.

The law relating to landownership is based on the original 11th-century feudal system, when there was a pyramid of land tenancy, each 'vassal' holding land from his 'superior'. The superior could put heavy constraints on the way that the vassal used the land.

Although long defunct, certain elements of the feudal system remain in relation to the law. In particular, no one actually 'owns' land today – they only 'hold' the land from the Crown. (However, the fact that the feudal system no longer operates means that they effectively own it.) In Scotland the system lasted for longer, although it has mainly been abolished since the 1970s. Only those houses and flats which have not changed hands since 1974 will be affected by this.

Another legacy of feudalism is that it is often only the actual owner (or leaseholder) who will be seen by the courts as having any right to sue for any violation of the rights he has over the land. This is rapidly changing in many areas of the law, now that it is recognised that husband and wife often own property jointly. Also in some cases full rights are given now to those who occupy premises but own no share of them. There are still some loopholes that need to be filled.

Spouses who have no part in the ownership can protect their right to occupy a matrimonial home by registering a 'charge' at the Land Registry, so that the spouse who actually owns the property cannot sell it and leave the other homeless.

Problem-solving methods

Many of these issues can be very complex; you may require the help of a solicitor if you feel that your rights are being violated. This book aims to cover the basic facts so that you can see if you have any case at all before spending money on legal advice. Remember the courts are not the only method of settling problems: if you cannot manage yourself, then your local council or the police can intervene.

In the end the law is only one small aspect of resolving any dispute that arises in relation to your home. Common sense, objectivity and a certain amount of cool-headedness are the main requirements for solving problems.

As Abraham Lincoln said: 'Discourage litigation, persuade your neighbours to compromise whenever you can. Point out to them how the nominal winner is often a loser in fees, expenses and cost of time.'

CHAPTER 1

The Extent of Your Property

An important part of establishing your rights is first to be sure what land you actually own, and in what way you own it.

FREEHOLDS AND LEASEHOLDS

Landownership in Britain is rather strange and complex because there has never been absolute ownership of land by an individual. This evolved from feudal days, when the King owned all the land in the country, and people were entitled to 'hold' the land – either on freehold or leasehold.

Freehold (or 'feudal tenure' in Scotland) gives the 'owner' the right to hold the land for ever or until it is sold again or given away in a will, so one can say freeholders are landowners.

Leasehold is the right to hold the land from the freeholder or another leaseholder (the landlord) for a certain amount of time, or until the freeholder serves a notice on the tenant to leave the property. A leasehold is usually for a fixed period, which might be anything from six months to 999 years.

It might offer a) the right to renew the lease when that time ends, or b) the right to buy the freehold from the landlord.

Leaseholds can also exist from week to week or month to month, just by a regular payment of rent to the landlord (*see* Chapter 5, Letting Your Home).

The rights and obligations outlined in this book mostly apply to both freeholders and leaseholders, with exceptions which will be covered.

FREEHOLDERS

The most important thing to look at is the title deeds. These are the documents that state that you own the property, and they therefore have to state as precisely as possible what you do own. If you own registered land (which most people do) then there will be a plan of the property at the Land Registry in Plymouth or the Register of Land in Edinburgh. This plan is likely to be less precise than the deeds, however, so you should look at the deeds first.

Unfortunately, deeds often leave the exact line of the boundary undetermined, because it is thought that the cost and time involved in defining the boundary precisely outweigh the rather small chances that such precision will be needed. If there is a boundary dispute then there are methods by which the precise ownership can be established, some of which are outlined here. If you really need to know the precise boundaries to your property, it might be best to see a solicitor.

What freeholders can do with their property

Although you may own your home until you choose to sell it, you are not allowed to do absolutely anything you want with it.

If you want to make changes to your property, it may well be that you need planning permission from the council (*see* Chapter 6, Making Changes to Your Home).

In deed

The deeds normally describe the property in the most commonsensical way available, using natural objects or measurements, such as fences, hedges or roads. This is often supplemented with a plan, though plans are rarely conclusive as to the precise position of the boundaries of the property.

CHECK this before deciding:
- to knock anything down or build anything new
- to change the use of your house (for example, from a home to a business, or conversion into flats).

The planning authority will take into account particularly how much the changes are likely to affect the neighbourhood and the neighbours. Once you have permission, if it is needed, then it is your choice as to whether you go ahead with the changes or not.

The previous owners of your home may have made a deal with the owners or previous owners of the next-door property, agreeing that certain things would not be done to either property. Even though the properties may have changed hands several times, it is likely that these agreements, known as 'restrictive covenants', can still be enforced by the present owners. Any past deals should have been pointed out when you bought the property, but to see if there are any existing you can check with the Land Registry in Plymouth or the Register of Land in Edinburgh if you own Scottish property; or check in the title deeds. Scottish properties may have extensive 'real burden and conditions' attached to the owner's rights over the property, which work in a similar way to restrictive covenants in England and Wales.

Your house may well be subject to a mortgage. Technically, the bank, building society or loan agency owns a proportion of the whole of your property, and so they would be able to object if you did anything which they thought devalued the property. You would need to talk to them first or check any conditions in the mortgage agreement.

Spouses have a right to reside in the property even where they do not own a share in it. It would not be possible to sell the matrimonial home upon divorce if the other partner had nowhere else to go, even if they had no share in the property.

However, there is usually little trouble in selling the property or making any improvements to it that you wish. Any expenses incurred in improving it can be reflected in the price you choose to ask should you eventually decide to sell your home.

LEASEHOLDERS/TENANTS

Conditions of a lease

The freeholder of the property agrees to give up for the time being, in return for rent, his rights to the property, in favour of someone else, subject to certain conditions. The tenant adopts all the rights that the landlord had before the lease, subject to the terms of the lease, and the fact that the landlord will at some point in the future reclaim his property.

During the period of the lease, the landlord deprives himself of the property so that he would actually be trespassing if he went onto it without the tenant's permission or under a clause of the lease. The same relationship may exist between a tenant and a subtenant (where the original tenant has let out a period of his lease to someone else).

- If your lease is in the form of a document, look there to find out what property you have rights over. The description of what has been leased to you should be relatively accurate, and will generally extend to everything the freeholder owns and is able to lease out to you. If there is no such description, it is generally safe to assume that you hold as much of the leased property as the landlord owns as a freeholder. (However, tenants do not take any mining rights in the land concerned!)
- You may have a long leasehold on your flat, for 21 years or longer if you live in England, especially London; this becomes similar to ownership under freehold. A lease of this length confers special rights on the leaseholder, such as buying the freehold or extending of the lease. In Scotland, however, landlords are not allowed to grant leases on dwelling houses for more than 20 years and so these rights do not apply.
- You may have no written lease. This can only occur when the lease is for less than three years (one year in Scotland), or when there is no fixed period of time that the lease will run for. This does not affect your rights as a tenant, except that it is a little more difficult to establish exactly where you stand.
- You may not have what the law officially recognises to be a lease, even

though you are renting somewhere to live from a freeholder or another leaseholder. If the property that you are paying rent for is granted to you by way of a licence, then you do not actually 'hold' the property and your rights over it are very limited.

Licences
These are found mainly
- in English law
- where the landlord is not legally restricted in any way from coming on to your property
- where the time period for your use of the property is unclear
- where there are lodgers

CHECK If you have any doubt as to whether you have a lease or a licence, *see* Chapter 5, Letting Your Home, before assuming that you have the rights normally granted to leaseholders.

Whether the lease was written or unwritten, the landlord can choose which parts of the property he wants to let, and which he does not. The parts that you do hold belong to you for the time being, subject to any exceptions in the lease that the landlord specified when he leased the property to you.

What the leaseholder can do with the property
The landlord will get the property back sometime in the future unless you choose to exercise any right to buy the freehold. The lease allows you to hold the land only for the time being, and not to treat it as though it were yours for ever.

With a written lease, the landlord probably will have stipulated what you cannot do, rather than what you can do to the property. For example – you might well be precluded from letting out the property yourself to a subtenant, (although in the absence of any such clause you are entitled to arrange a sublet as long as that sublease comes to an end before your own lease).

Alterations and improvements

Leases often include a general clause stating that the tenant cannot make substantial alterations to the property without the landlord's consent. This is because the property will, at some point in the future, come back into the ownership of the landlord, and he does not want it devalued in the meantime.

Remember You do need to be careful about any improvements you make to the property while it is yours. This is not a problem for freeholders, since improvements can be taken into account in the asking price when the property is sold, or perhaps removed from the land if they are to be transferred to the freeholder's next house. But as a tenant you should be aware that many improvements you make while the lease is in force may well transfer to the landlord when that lease expires.

Exceptions You are allowed some freedom to make changes to the property without eventually giving your landlord the benefit of your expenses and efforts.

- You can take objects away when you leave which, although they appear to have become part of the house or the land, are for the purposes of your trade, or are decorations.
- If you put in a phone line for a private or residential purpose, the landlord will probably get the benefit of it when you leave, unless you were able to come to some agreement with him or her regarding the cost. But you would be entitled to take any wallpaper you put up when your lease expired (although it wouldn't be much good to you by then and you might have to compensate him for any damage you do when removing it!).
- Any improvements which do not come under trade or decorations become your landlord's property when the lease ends; however they will become yours again if your lease is renewed immediately.

Flats or apartments

The conveyance (deeds) or the lease should describe accurately what is to

belong to you, even though the flat may form only part of a building.
Generally you will own or lease

- all of the external walls
- your side of any internal partition walls
- all the space from your floor up to the bottom of the floor in the flat
  above.

Many flats in England are owned on long leasehold (more than 21 years),
but with a right to extend the lease or buy the freehold. It is the actual land
rather than the buildings that you buy on freehold, and so if tenants wish
to buy the freehold of the block of flats that they live in, they will have to
club together and share it. This can be done either by a trust, where up to
four of the tenants actually own the freehold, but hold it on trust for the
others (no more than four people can jointly own property in their own
names), by setting up a company in which everyone has shares.

Maintenance and repairs of the common parts of the block of flats can
then be administered through the trust or company.

Flats in Scotland Flats are normally owned rather than leased and the
ownership of various parts of the block or property will usually be outlined
in the deeds. (In the absence of any such provisions the old law of
tenement will apply, but this is very rare). Most Scottish deeds provide

---

Common ground

Remember that it is only the flat that you actually live in which is yours
to hold. There will normally be common parts to the building which will
not belong to you under the lease, such as the hallway to the building
your flat is in. For instance, if there are several flats in one building, the
common parts may include the front door, the entrance hall, the staircase
going up to the flats, and the roof space on top of the building. It is the
landlord who continues to own these areas rather than you, although you
will have a right to walk through the front door of the building and the
hallway or staircase, if this is necessary for you to get to your flat.

that all the flat owners share common parts such as the roof and stairways, and have to contribute to its upkeep between themselves. Where there is a lack of cooperation about this even by just one of the flat-owners, the council has the power to step in and sort the problem out.

Scottish flat-owners therefore rely much more on cooperation for the upkeep of the common parts of their property, living rather as a commune in this respect. This is mainly because Scottish leases are restricted to a maximum of 20 years, so that many more properties are held on feudal tenure than leases.

Council tenancies

These are just like normal leases in terms of what you hold, and what you can do with the property, although the council as landlord can impose its own terms in the leases (subject to a number of limits).

THE OUTER LIMITS OF YOUR PROPERTY

Your ownership in theory extends infinitely up into the sky and down into the centre of the earth along the boundaries, as far as they can be ascertained, and so the ownership is three-dimensional. However, this does not give you absolute rights to anything that is in the sky or in the earth.

For instance, your right to airspace only really extends to what you actually need for the purposes of living in your home, and may be restricted if building an extra floor means that you will deprive a neighbour of any 'right to light', or if you contravene planning regulations. *See* Chapter 2, People on Your Property, and Chapter 6, Making Changes to Your Home.

Boundaries

A common problem is the question of who actually owns the boundary structures, such as walls and fences, that are used to describe the extent of the property. However, this is only an issue when the wall, fence or hedge falls on the boundary itself, and not just inside one of the adjacent properties.

Walls

Often the ownership of the boundary structures is stated in the deeds or lease – for example, 'up to and including . . . .' Otherwise the general rule to follow is if there is an external wall which does not form part of your next-door neighbour's wall, then you own all of that external wall. But if the edge of the property is an internal wall, then you own the half of the wall that is on your side.

Where a dispute develops between you and your neighbour regarding an internal party wall, it is best to come to an agreement that you both own half of it which can be simply drawn up and signed between the two of you. Where you are unable to agree on this, the court can make a declaration as to ownership of the party wall. This may be cheaper than having to go to court to fight any dispute that results from your disagreement.

GENERAL RULE the portion of a party wall on each side of an imaginary vertical line drawn through the middle is owned by the corresponding owner.

There may still be obligations to the owner of the other side of the wall, where the structure of their house depends partly on buildings on your land. So in terraced houses and flats there is a 'right of support' in the other side of the wall to your property.

Party walls in England and Wales

1 If your neighbour's half of the party wall falls into a state of disrepair, which damages or threatens to damage your property or your half of the party wall, then you are entitled to go on to his property and repair the damage.

Remember

- You will have no right of action in the courts against him.
- He is not liable for damages if there has been damage.
- You will not be able to get an injunction against him if the condition of his side of the wall threatens damage.

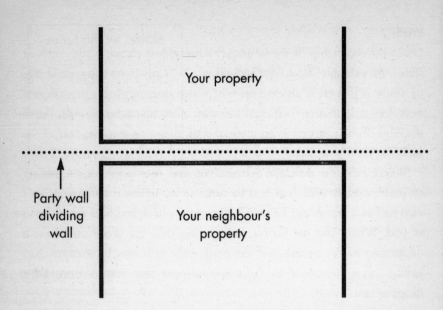

- You cannot force your neighbour to undertake the repairs that are necessary. You can do them yourself – but you are not entitled to recover the cost of these repairs from him unless there is a specific agreement between you.

2 If your neighbour deliberately knocks down their wall, threatening or causing damage to your property, you are entitled to
- an injunction to stop them pulling the wall down
- compensation for any damage that is actually done to your building. They will be liable to pay even though builders in their employ pulled the wall down. They are also liable to pay even if they sell the property on to someone else before all the damage has happened to your property. You have the same rights against the council if they do this to one of their properties, or a property in their care.

3 If your neighbour allows something to happen to the party wall which he knows about, or might reasonably be expected to know about, which may cause damage to your side of the party wall, the situation is less clear. (This is not the same as where the wall on his side disintegrates

due to age, or falls down unexpectedly.) Generally you have the same rights as if the neighbour had done a positive act such as knocking down the wall, since it is his fault that this state of affairs arose.

> **Sitting on the fence**
>
> If there is no next-door neighbour, and the other side of the fence is just waste land, the law presumes that you own the entire fence.

For example, if dry rot or damp starts from his side of the wall and can be seen there, this will normally give you a right of action if it threatens the structure of your side; you can get an injunction against him or recover compensation for the damage.

It may be clear occasionally from the title deeds that either you or your neighbours own the entire dividing wall. Here the person who does not own the wall will still have a 'right of support', in case any damage to the wall threatens the structure of any part of the rest of the property. But the limits to what you can do still apply.

Party walls in Scotland

In Scotland, all those whose house structure depends upon the structure of another are said to have a 'common interest' in the other property. If you own a terraced house or flat you have some say in what your neighbour chooses to do with his property; this applies if there is a substantial risk that it will affect your property, whether he acts deliberately or through neglect regarding the condition of the wall.

You could seek interdict (injunct) against him from taking a positive action such as knocking down a supporting wall. If neglect by the ground-floor flat-owner causes that flat to fall into disrepair, you can either seek interdict (injunction) against him before any damage actually occurs, or claim compensation for any damage and repairs to your flat after the event. If it is not his fault, or he could not have known that his flat was falling into disrepair, for example when a beam that supports the ceiling fractures unexpectedly after time, then, as in England and Wales, he will not be liable.

Fences and hedges

Where it is clear that a fence or hedge is placed on one side of the boundary, it is generally the rule that it belongs to the person who owns the land on that side of the boundary. If the fence appears to fall exactly on the boundary, you and your neighbour may agree either you will both share responsibility for it, or that one or other of you owns it outright.

If in doubt you should look to see what degree of responsibility either of you has taken for the fence in the past.

- Has either of you painted (both sides of) the fence or regularly clipped (both sides of) the hedge?
- Has either of you repaired it or did either of you build the fence or plant the hedge in the first place?

This all affects who might be regarded as the owner, or whether the fence or hedge might be deemed to be shared between you. Avoid fruitless and expensive court battles; it is never worth arguing over a fence or a hedge to such an extent, and an agreement should be reached if at all possible.

If you built the fence just over your boundary and on your neighbour's land by mistake, technically this is an act of trespass (*see* Chapter 2, People on Your Property, and Chapter 3, Trouble with Your Neighbours). Your neighbour has the right to dismantle the fence and reclaim possession of his land. However, if the fence has been there for 12 years or more (10 years or more in Scotland), and you have used the land inside it as though it were your own for that time, you have won the land concerned from your neighbour.

Roads and pavements

If a public road marks the end of your property, the surface of the road and pavement is owned by your local council. It also owns 'so much of the soil beneath as is necessary for the authority to perform its statutory duties' (for example, repairing the road). Technically, you will probably own the subsoil up to the middle of the road, and so you would be entitled to build a cellar under the road, providing you got approval from the council in terms of the structural requirements.

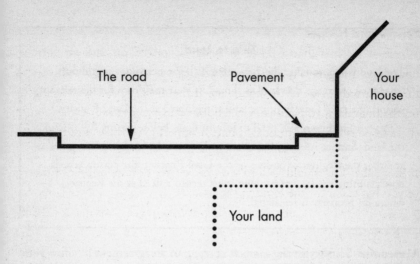

A public road includes the edge of the pavement nearest to your property, for example – a wall to your front garden or your house, or the end of your lawn. Sometimes the council owns some of the land beyond the edge of the pavement, so check your deeds. The path to your front door belongs to you, although almost anyone has a right to use it if they are coming up to knock on your door for a lawful purpose (*see* Chapter 2, People on Your Property).

Changing boundaries

If the owners of the property next door (including both previous and current owners) have extended their garden into what is technically your land, such as by placing a fence too far over the boundary, then after 12 years (ten in Scotland) of the fence being in that place, the fence and everything contained within the incursion become part of the next-door property.

This process by which property changes hands can seem unfair, although it can work to your advantage. It may be effected by actions such as planting flowers or bushes in the area of land taken over, or parking cars regularly on your land as though it were their own land, for a total of ten or 12 continuous years, depending on whether the property is in Scotland or in England or Wales.

Title to land

The land will automatically change hands if the next-door neighbours have gone on to use that land as though it were their own for the relevant period of time. However, if the land is registered at the Land Registry, then your neighbour will need to inform them before getting full title to the land. Similar rules apply in Scotland, where the land will be registered at either the Register of Sasines or the Land Register; the person who is now claiming the land as his own must record a deed at the Register where his property is registered.

Remember This is not the same as coming to an agreement to allow your neighbour to plant the flowers or park his cars on your land, while acknowledging that the land remains yours. In that situation there would be no change of ownership.

WHAT YOU OWN WITHIN YOUR PROPERTY

The ownership of objects and material on your property can be very relevant when it comes to selling or leasing your house, since disputes may arise over what parts of the property can be transferred to the next owner. If your rights over these are not stated in the deeds, you must look at what the law considers to be part of the land you own.

Fixtures

There are two factors to consider here.

Anything physically attached to the land or the house becomes part of the land that you hold or own. To determine whether something is physically attached consider whether it could be removed from the land or the building without causing any damage. A structure such as a free-standing greenhouse or hut, which is not actually fixed to the land, may well be seen as independent and therefore still belonging to the person who originally put it there (unless of course it was specifically sold with the house).

Example You might have:

- A hut in your garden which rests on sockets drilled into the soil. Although the sockets are physically attached, the hut itself could be removed without damaging the land, and so it would not be seen by the law as being part of the land that you bought or leased.
- A greenhouse attached to a concrete slab merely resting on the property by virtue of its own weight, to which the same rule applies.

The original reason for the object being put on your land must also be examined:

- If it was part of a permanent scheme of design or layout of the property then it is probably considered to be part of the land. So even if the object is not physically attached to the land, and is only held in position by its own weight, the question of whether it forms part of the architectural design of the house or garden is an important consideration.
- It may be that something is physically attached to the property, purely for the enjoyment of the object itself, and forms no essential part of the design of the house.
- If it is there merely to display itself, then it is not part of the property; but if it is there because it fits into the more general display of the property as a whole, then it is considered to be part of the property. In 1902 it was decided that even though a tapestry was attached to a wall of the house by nails and tacks, it was not an integral part of the decor or architecture, and therefore not part of the property.

Remember if you are selling a property and wish to take a certain fixture with you: you must make it clear to your intended purchaser that you wish to take something in particular, for example a shrub in the garden or a carefully chosen light fitting.

Safety

Although it is up to the company or builder who installs pipes or wires to do so competently, always check that they are safe, since you as the owner

---

Telephone, electricity, gas and water

Telephone and electricity wires, gas and water pipes become part of your property once they are installed, although only if they are for the supply of services to your house. A landlord might choose to reserve them in the lease, so that they remain his responsibility. Overhead cables and underground pipes remain the property of the electricity company, British Telecom or British Gas.

---

may also be held responsible for any fire or leaks that result. Any subsequent interference by you may well lead to you being liable for the consequences of any escape of gas. This includes the interference by an independent contractor employed by you; you therefore need to check that the work he has done is competent.

Summary

1 Is the object attached to the property to the extent that removing it would cause some damage to the land or the building to which it is attached?

2 Is the object part of some permanent improvement to the land, which forms part of the whole design of the property?

Remember some things that appear to come with the property, whether attached to the land or not, might be specifically excluded in your lease or title deeds, and vice versa.

Scotland

Consideration will also be given to how much the object weighs. For example, a large summerhouse may be considered a fixture in Scotland even though it just rests on the ground without actually being attached to anything. Scottish courts take into account whether the land was specially adapted in any way to accommodate the object – if special work has been done it is more likely to be treated as part of the land.

Trees

If the trunk and roots of a tree grow to extend over the boundary the person who owns the land on which it was originally planted still owns all of the tree.

Where ownership is disputed, look to see who has tended the tree in the past. If the previous owners of the property did this, the tree will have passed to the new owner of the land. *See* overhanging trees and branches, page 48.

Buried treasure

Everyone dreams of finding lost treasure on their property! In England and Wales, however, there are some considerations which apply if anything of interest or value is discovered in your garden, despite the fact that you are supposed to own everything underneath your property to the centre of the earth.

- Treasure that was buried by someone many years ago who intended to come back to it later, automatically belongs to the Monarch.
- You are obliged to report the find to the local coroner (through your local police station) and hand the property over to him.
- You will receive the full market price as the finder if it is kept for a museum or for the Crown. If it is not kept by them, it will be returned to you and you can keep it.
- Treasure that is just lost or abandoned, is yours to keep, again as the finder rather than the owner of the land on which it was discovered.

If in doubt Report it to the coroner who will decide whether it is lost or buried, since you can be imprisoned for failing to declare buried treasure.

The 'finders keepers' rule does not apply to situations where it can be deduced or discovered who the owner is. Where the object found obviously belongs to someone, you ought to try to find the owner; treating that object as one's own would otherwise be theft. However, the finder generally has more rights to own the object than anyone else except the actual owner of the object.

The owner of the land on which the object was found might be able to

Mineral rights

Certain minerals have their own rules. Minerals in general belong to the owner of the land (or leaseholder, unless prevented by a clause in the lease) directly above, but gold, silver and petroleum oil – the most valuable minerals – belong to the Crown when they are in the mineral state (as opposed to gold treasure, which might have been lost or buried). All coal belongs to British Coal, and all natural gas belongs to the Crown. Unfortunately, the Crown doesn't have to compensate you with the equivalent market value for this.

claim ownership, as might the tenant, unless the landlord has specifically excluded the tenant's right to lost property found on the land in the lease.

The landowner has more rights of ownership
• where the finder was a trespasser on the land when he found the object
• where the property was buried in the land
• where the landowner has a strong measure of control over the land concerned.

In a private garden it is likely that the owner of the garden would have a better claim to the object than the finder, but in a field or a wood (if the finder is not trespassing) the finder has more rights of ownership than the landowner.

Scotland

All lost or buried treasure belongs to the crown and all lost or abandoned property that is found must be taken to the police station 'without reasonable delay', even if the property is found on the finder's own land. The police will attempt to find the owners, although if they are unsuccessful after two months, then they may return the property to the finder.

CHAPTER 2

People on Your Property

Much of English and Scottish land law is based on the days when owning land was one of the most important status symbols. The rights that come with landownership reflect the respect that the law has for those in this position. Among these is the right to exclude anyone you do not wish to cross your boundaries, or anything that belongs to other people which you do not want on your property.

So what can you do when people come on to your property without your permission?

TRESPASSING

A person coming on to your property without your permission (whether you own the property or lease it) constitutes a trespass to your property, even if they cause no trouble, harm or damage. Trespass is not a criminal matter, but the law allows you to exert your rights as a property owner against a trespasser.

- You can order a trespasser to leave, and if they refuse you can use a certain amount of force to eject them.
- The courts will back you up if you find that a certain person or group of people is trespassing regularly on your property, despite your attempts to let them know that they cannot come on to it without your permission.

What happens when someone else who is living fulltime at the house wants to invite someone in, against the wishes of the owner or

---

The person in possession

Those who can give permission for someone to come on to any privately owned property are:

- all people who own the property, or share the ownership (unless the property has been let under a lease).
- the leaseholder, or those who share the lease of the property, if the property has been let under a lease.

Lodgers and people who do not have a proper lease are in a weaker position; it is only your landlord who has a right against trespassers.

See Leaseholders/Tenants, page 14; Rights and obligations of landlords and tenants, page 89.

---

leaseholder? Who does the law view as the 'occupier' at the time of the incident? And who gets to decide when there is a disagreement between the 'occupiers'?

Currently in law it is still only the actual owner, or person in whose name the lease is made, who can decide. However, if a situation came to court today in which a spouse with no property rights wanted to sue someone for trespass to the place that he or she lived in, it is most likely that a court would allow him or her, or perhaps any grown-up children living there as well, a right to sue in trespass.

Example If a husband owned the property outright, and his wife wanted a particular friend to come round whom the husband objected to, the husband could do nothing to stop that friend entering the property. The friend would not be a trespasser so long as he or she has the permission to be there from someone who lives at the property. The wife in these circumstances has a right to occupy the matrimonial home which is guaranteed by Parliament; she cannot be evicted by her husband as a trespasser on the property. This right may also be registered at the Land Registry in Plymouth or the Register of Land in Edinburgh to protect the wife against the home being sold from underneath her by her husband.

Example If the person who owns the property (say the husband) deserts his spouse, leaving her in a house she does not own, there is a 'sliding scale' of property rights, depending on how close the couple remain. Once they are totally separated, only the wife would be able to decide who came into the property. It is unlikely that she would ever be able totally to exclude the husband, who is after all the owner of the property. However, he should only be able to come to the house for good reasons, and he could not give permission for others to come in. And if all he wanted to do was harass her or cause trouble, a court would probably grant the wife an injunction to stop him doing this.

Much of the law still works on the basis that there is only one breadwinner in any family to own property – there is much catching up to do.

Although only the 'occupier' can give permission to people to come on to their property, certain people may have implied permission to do certain things; for instance, the postman is allowed to come up to your front door to deliver the letters, and a policeman can enter if he believes that there is a breach of the peace taking place inside your house. (*See* People who have a right to come on to your property, page 37).

The nature of trespass
Trespass itself is only a civil wrong, rather than a crime; normally it is a matter for you to deal with, although the police might be able to help if the situation becomes more serious. (*See* Burglary and other crimes by trespassers, page 36).

Trespass applies to:
* people voluntarily, and without the occupier's consent, coming on to your property.

Remember Your property constitutes a 3D area, not just the ground, but also some airspace above it. *See* The outer limits of your property, page 18.

Up in the air

Although your property extends in theory upwards for ever and down to the centre of the earth, an aircraft is rarely trespassing on your property unless it is flying at an unreasonably low height. The Ministry of Defence normally takes care in deciding where to practise military exercises, although there will be little that you can do in law to make them stop regular low-flying training in your area. However, do not hesitate to write to them if they become unbearable.

- people deliberately placing or throwing something onto your property, such as dumping rubbish without permission.

See Chapter 3, Trouble with Your Neighbours.

The law is strict when it comes to trespass and it only takes the slightest entry on to your property to constitute a wrong. Even putting a foot in your door or standing on your window ledge would amount to a trespass if you had not given the person permission to come on to your property. All that is required is that he or she intended to come on to your land.

It is no excuse for the trespasser to say that he thought he could come into your house or onto your land but was merely mistaken, or even that he did not know that it was private property.

Exceptions
- If someone else who was not the 'occupier' of the house (for the purposes of being able to give permission to come in) gave permission, and the visitor had good reason for believing that this person could give permission, then he would not be trespassing until the real occupier came along and withdrew that permission.

Example a salesman came to your door while you were out, but a friend was in your house with your permission and let the salesman in to see what he had to offer. Although the salesman did not have permission to come in from you, he would not be trespassing if he thought that your friend was able to give him such permission.

- Someone being carried or pushed into a home when she or he did not have the occupier's permission to come in would not be trespassing, as long as they left when they had the opportunity to do so. The point is that it was not the trespasser's intention to come into the home.

Summary

Trespass applies to unwanted guests and other intruders, so that any invitation to someone to come into your home can be withdrawn at any time you choose. Once you ask someone to leave, they have as much time as it takes them to collect their coat or other belongings and get out of the door before they become a trespasser.

Remember it is your permission as the owner or the leaseholder which determines whether the guest is trespassing or not. If two people own the house and only one gives permission, then the guest cannot be expelled from the house by the other person. You can qualify your permission by saying that he can only go into certain rooms in your house, or stay in the garden, or at the front door. Should he then try to go into other parts of the house, he would be trespassing.

What you can do about trespassers

Dealing with trespassers who refuse to leave is not straightforward.

Your primary right against trespassers is that you can order them to leave, but if you find that the person you have asked to leave refuses to do so, you are entitled to become slightly more physical.

Be very careful when you decide to resort to this, though. If you use any more force than would be deemed reasonably necessary to get the trespasser out of the house, you will be liable to him in damages for assault and battery, and ultimately could face a criminal charge.

You must also be absolutely sure that he is a trespasser before trying to throw him out. If it turns out that he was allowed to be there, you are unlawfully assaulting him (an assault can be the merest touch or even just

---

Dealing with squatters

You are not entitled to use force to get squatters out of your property (even though they are basically trespassers), nor a former tenant who refuses to leave the property once his lease has expired. It may be that the police will help you to get rid of the squatters where it is obvious that they are not entitled to be there, especially where they have damaged or stolen any of your property. But if there is any doubt then you will need an order of the court. *See* Chapter 7, Resolving Disputes.

---

a threat) and once again you could be liable to him in damages or even face a criminal charge.

Where he is using force or violence to get into your house, it will be obvious that he is trespassing. In these circumstances you do not strictly have to ask him verbally to leave before you use force to get him out. However, you should still give him the chance to go, and you must then only use the force that is necessary for the purpose of getting him out. The principles of self-defence may apply, in which case you are still only allowed to use such force as is reasonably necessary in the circumstances, although these circumstances may warrant the use of slightly more force.

'Reasonably necessary force' is a well-used legal phrase which is complicated to define. It is made all the more difficult to apply because in these situations, there often is not enough time to consider what would be reasonably necessary. A court would take this into account, but is conscious that many people in these circumstances are prone to losing their temper, and may therefore use more force than is necessary. Anything the court would view as excessive constitutes assault.

Example There is an unwanted guest on your premises. You ask him to leave your property, thus leaving no doubt that he does not have your permission. If he refuses, you should warn him that you will forcibly throw him off the property if he does not go. Should he still refuse, you might take hold of him and push him towards the door. He may change his stance and agree to go while you are doing this, in which case you should let go of him, not forgetting that he is entitled to collect any of his belongings first. If he uses force back at you, you can use self-defence, but no more force than is necessary to defend yourself.

Unfortunately, a policeman has no duty to help you get rid of trespassers unless the trespasser is committing an offence at the time. But you might be able to get some help if you are being harassed. (*See* Harassment, page 44). You are only entitled at this stage to get the trespasser out of the house, you cannot stop him from leaving. Nor can you arrest someone for it, since simple trespassing is not a crime.

Other options

Technically you can sue for damages, but this would only be worthwhile if the trespasser actually caused damage to anything you could put a price on. Otherwise, you would only receive nominal damages (such as £1) since the court would take a dim view of your having gone to so much trouble over such a small matter.

A more useful remedy is an injunction, where you believe that the trespass is likely to happen again and become a regular occurrence, especially if you have good reason for not letting him or her into your house or on to your land. A particularly good reason might be that he or she is harassing you or your family, but as a matter of law you are entitled

---

Self-defence or punishment?

In November 1993 Ted Newbury shot a suspected burglar as his own way of saying 'get off my property' and was ordered to pay the burglar £4,000 compensation for the injuries that were caused. If Mr Newbury had warned the burglar that he had a gun, or maybe even fired a warning shot in a direction that could not possibly have hit anyone, then there should have been no more trouble. If the burglar had not left despite this warning, Mr Newbury might have believed his life to be in danger. He then might have been justified in injuring the burglar to protect himself, but not as some form of punishment.

to an injunction whether the trespasser is causing you trouble or not. *See* Harassment, page 44.

Burglary and other crimes by trespassers

Trespass is a crime where it involves violent or forcible entry, where the trespasser has a weapon, or where he is a burglar. Burglary is a matter of combining trespass with either committing a criminal offence or intending to commit one. The criminal offences that would make his trespass constitute burglary are theft, grievous bodily harm, rape or criminal damage.

It is important to distinguish burglary and other crimes from simple trespass, since the potential solutions are slightly different.

- You are entitled to use self-defence against him if he attacks or threatens to attack you.
- If you believe that the trespasser has committed a criminal offence (whether as a burglar or otherwise) or is intending to commit an offence, you can use some force in the prevention of the crime, but, again that force will be only what would be considered reasonably necessary to stop the crime.

Remember The best thing to do if you suspect that you have a burglar on your premises is to call the police rather than try to tackle him yourself. As a burglar he might be prepared to take far greater measures, since he faces more serious consequences.

Protecting your property

Although you wish to keep out people who might invade your personal space, whether trespassers or burglars, you have to be careful that what you do does not constitute an assault.

Dogs You are allowed to deter burglars by saying you have a large dog whether you do or do not actually own one. However, you cannot use a guard dog on your premises without a proper dog-handler or a licence.

'Guard dog' here means a dog that is allowed to roam free rather than being kept in the house or the kennel or tied up.

Deterrents   You are not allowed to set positive traps that might injure anyone, even if that person would probably be breaking the law at the time. The limit of any action that you can take might be some broken glass or spikes on top of a high wall, provided that these can be seen from the ground in the daylight. However, as by putting spikes or broken glass on a wall that you know people regularly climb on to (perhaps children playing games) you would be taking a risk that they would be injured, you would be liable for any injury to them. Also the wall must be high enough so that passers-by are not going to catch themselves or their clothing on whatever you put on the wall.

PEOPLE WHO HAVE A RIGHT TO COME ON TO YOUR PROPERTY

In certain circumstances, people can come on to your property without your express permission, and these people are not trespassing.

Public rights of way

There might be a public right of way or footpath over your property, which ought to have been clearly marked by the council. If it causes you substantial inconvenience, you might be able to apply to the council to have the public right of way removed.

Remember   many public rights of way have been established over many years, and it is likely that you will just have to live with it. Any member of the public can enforce a right of way in the courts, although it is most likely that the matter will be taken up by the local council, at least to start with.

> **Grouse scarers**
>
> In 1893 the Duke of Rutland obtained an injunction against anti-blood sports demonstrators who used a public right of way across his land to scare the grouse away from the guns.

However, people are only entitled to use the right of way as it is defined.

- They are not allowed to come off the footpath and on to your property.
- They are only entitled to use it as a footpath. Anything they do beyond that, even if it does not involve coming off the footpath, constitutes trespass to the owner of the land.

Hedges and trees The hedges and trees that grow along the side of the right of way still belong to you and are your responsibility – they must therefore be trimmed and looked after by you. Sometimes, however, the local council may agree to do this for you. As regards the footpath itself, you do not have obligations concerning the safety of the path's users in the same way that you have obligations to most visitors to your property. *See* Chapter 4, Your Obligations as a Homeowner. The state of the footpath will therefore be the responsibility of the local authority.

Danger on your property

People, not just the police, can enter your property if it is necessary to prevent injury to people or damage to property. This is not a carte blanche to enter your property, though, since any such threat to people or property must be imminent, so that the rescuer has no option other than to enter your premises.

Neighbours carrying out repairs

Nuisance Your neighbour may sometimes have the right to go on to your property if something on it constitutes what is known as a nuisance to him. For example, if you have let your side of a party wall fall into disrepair, and its condition threatens his side of the wall or any other part of his property, he is entitled to go onto your property to repair it. This is known as his right of abatement of nuisance, and will be examined in terms of your rights against him. *See* What to do if you anticipate damage, page 65.

Building works If your neighbour is carrying out some works to his house, which makes it necessary, or substantially more convenient for him, to come on to your property, it is possible for him to get a court order permitting this. For instance it might be that he can only get to his roof or to a certain drain from the roof of your house.

Of course, it is much easier for everyone if you can come to some arrangement to do this. If you cannot, however, the court can give your neighbour permission to go on to your property, unless the court thinks that it will be too hard on you. It might be that the work will take several days, and that he will need to keep some materials on your property in the meantime. The court may wish him to pay you some compensation for any inconvenience and loss of privacy that you may suffer, he will also have to pay for any damage caused to your property by his works.

Sometimes the right for a neighbour to come on to your property to carry out works on his property is part of the rights that come with ownership of his property. This right may be specifically mentioned in the title deeds to either property, or it may arise out of necessity or common sense.

Neighbours' rights of way

Your neighbour might have a right of way over your property in order to get to his own property. His house may be behind yours and only accessible from a path which runs along the side of your house, but which is technically part of your property. Thus he will be able to use the right of way for all normal purposes of living there, including letting guests use it to get to his house.

However, he does not get all the benefits of ownership. It is up to you if you wish to resurface the path, although you will probably have to pay compensation to your neighbour while he cannot use his right of way, even though it is your property. You may come to an agreement whereby you share the cost of resurfacing or repairing the path. While the path is unusable, your neighbour will most likely be entitled to use another way through your property.

If you have leased out a flat at the top of your house and the tenant can only get to it by going up the staircase in the main part of the house, then your tenant has a right to use that staircase; a lodger would have the same rights.

This kind of right of way also applies when there is something on your property that your neighbour needs to get to in order to properly use his own home. For example, there may be an electricity meter which is on your property but serves the homes of several neighbours nearby. If they need to get to the meter themselves, they have the right to do so – but they should not use this right of way for any other purpose.

The police

The police have wider powers than most people to enter your property, but because they have to follow a strict code of conduct when investigating offences, these powers have been carefully defined. Police powers are therefore more limited than people think. A policeman can enter your property:

- for the purpose of arresting someone there whether he has a warrant for the arrest, or just believes that the person to be arrested is in your home. There is no right of sanctuary for criminals or suspected criminals in your home.
- if he is in the process of trying to capture a suspect at large, and you are under a duty to help the policeman do this if he asks you to.
- for the purpose of saving life or limb or preventing serious damage to any property. Therefore if it looks or sounds as though there is a breach of the peace going on in your home, the police are entitled to come on to your property to intervene. It does not matter whether there actually was a breach of the peace or not: the law is concerned with what the situation must have seemed like to the policeman when he was outside your house.

Once a policeman has entered your property, either under the rules set out above, or with your consent, he may take any property he sees which he believes would be evidence in any criminal proceedings. However:

- If it is something you don't want the police to hold, you can request that you keep it at home with you on their behalf, pending further investigation.

- If he is taking the property you are entitled to a receipt.
- The property can only be held at the police station for as long as the police actually need it.

The police may, for whatever reason, want to search your house for property that they suspect is connected with a criminal offence. They might apply for a search warrant from a magistrate (and then use reasonable force to get in if necessary), or ask you to consent to a search. Any consent to a search has to be in writing (for the police's protection rather than anything else).

Court bailiffs

It might be the case that you have had a judgement made against you for a sum of money in the county court. If you do not pay the plaintiff (see below) this money and the plaintiff then applies for execution of the judgement, the officers of the court have the right to take some of your property to the value of the sum of money involved. *See* Chapter 7, Resolving Disputes.

Remember the court officers (bailiffs) are not entitled to use force to gain entry to your property, so long as you do not let them in in the first place and then throw them out again later. If you let them in to your house then they are entitled to take the goods that they think suitable. But your front and back doors are safe if you refuse to let them in from the start.

But be aware that they are only safe if it is you and your property that the bailiff wants in relation to the court judgement. If someone else has a judgement against them, but decides to use your house to keep the property in, then the bailiff is entitled to use force to gain entry to your house. The bailiff might decide to come into your house to look for someone else's property, but if it turns out that no such property is there, you have a valid claim for trespass against the court.

Plaintiff: a person who brings a charge against somebody else in court.

Unfortunately, once the bailiff is in your home, he is entitled to break cases or cupboards open in order to search for relevant property, even if he has not asked you to open them first. In practice, such behaviour is extremely unlikely.

Council inspectors and other officials

Local authority inspectors and officers are permitted by statute to enter your home for the purposes of inspecting the premises or taking remedial action under the Public Health Act or any of the building regulations. They can come along during reasonable hours – 7am to 11pm. They can also go into your house if it is your next-door neighbour's house that they are concerned with, since that may be the only way to look at the problem in question.

If you refuse entry, you might be fined by a magistrates' court. The council inspectors can get a warrant from that court to authorise entry, which means that they are entitled to use force if you continue to refuse to let them in.

Planning inspectors have to give you 24 hours' notice should they wish to come into your home. However, they are entitled to use force to gain entry once that 24 hours has expired and it is an offence for you to obstruct them.

Representatives from the gas and electricity companies who have to enter your house in order to check the meter or do essential work on pipes or wires have a right to come into your home too. They also have rights of entry into your home and access on to your land to check that pipes and wires are in proper and safe working order. Where it is urgent, for instance when a gas leak is threatened, they are entitled to use force to come in.

Television licence inspectors need a warrant of entry and search of premises from a magistrate before they can come in.

You are entitled to ask for identification of their authority, and it is recommended that you do this.

Hawkers and tradesmen

Door-to-door salesmen are allowed to knock on your front or back door provided that you have not already said that they cannot do so.

- You can do this either by putting a sign outside your house saying something like 'No hawkers, traders, door-to-door salesmen' or by locking the gate to your front garden. Such actions would tell any salesman that you have cancelled his right to conduct his business on your premises.
- You can also cancel his right to do that once he has knocked on your door, and told you what he is selling. He should leave once you have revoked your permission. The same rules apply to policemen unless they have any of the special reasons for coming into your home already outlined.

Remember this right of hawkers only applies if the salesman is there for that purpose. When he has no lawful reason for knocking at your door, he will be a trespasser if he has come on to any part of your property. The hawker's right does not apply to personal investigators or inquiry agents!

Privacy in your home

There is no basic right to privacy in English law, although there has been much discussion recently about the possibility of introducing a privacy law, following the way some newspaper journalists go about trying to get their stories.

Privacy can cover many different circumstances, and it may be possible to protect your privacy in your home by a number of other means.

Bird's eye view

In 1978 Lord Bernstein failed to claim damages against an aerial photography company who had flown over his land (and therefore into his airspace) to take a photograph of the house. It was decided that since the aircraft was flying at a reasonable height, this did not constitute trespass, and so Lord Bernstein could do nothing about it. No legal wrong was being committed against him.

For instance, you might object to planning permission for your neighbour to build an extension to his house on the basis that it would give him a direct view into your bathroom window. *See* Chapter 6, Making Changes to Your Home.

There are other ways of stopping people interfering with your privacy, but you can only do this (whether by injunction or any other means) where they are committing a legal wrong against you that is established as a principle in law. Look back at advice given earlier in the chapter about trespassers; this might give you a remedy against a breach of privacy.

Harassment

Another form of invasion of privacy is when someone is constantly causing trouble by, say, telephoning you at all hours in order to annoy you, or regularly being offensive to you from the street while you are in your home.

What constitutes a legal wrong

- Causing or threatening to cause any damage to your property
- Causing or threatening to cause mental or physical injury to you
- Harassing you to the extent that your health might be impaired as you become more and more exasperated by the situation.

If you fear that someone is likely to trespass on your premises, or damage any of your property (such as your car), then you have a basis upon which to exert your rights. Where he or she has done any of these things in the past, you would have a good chance of obtaining an injunction against them, but precisely what you do about the problem is up to you – it might be the case that rising to their provocation will only cause more trouble. You might be able to persuade the police to warn your harasser off rather than go to court for an injunction.

Remember It would be difficult to get an injunction against someone in this respect unless the danger or actual damage is clear. However much you believe that the person might cause damage or injury to you, there would have to be clear evidence of something that he said or did to persuade a judge that an injunction could be justified.

If the trouble is coming from constant telephone calls, you can get an injunction to stop this if you know who is making the calls. However, for it to be actual harassment, the calls would have to be persistent, and at inconvenient times, such as in the evening or the middle of the night. Try to see it from the point of view of an objective person looking at your situation – as a judge might. Would it seem to him to be intolerable (or plain offensive, in the event of the calls being abusive)?

Alternatively, it might be worth trying to get British Telecom to monitor and interrupt your calls. There are now telephones which show you the number of the person trying to get through to you before you pick up the phone (though it is possible for someone to telephone without a phone number being given).

Examples of what behaviour might constitute harassment have only been properly brought before the courts in recent years. However, no tort of harassment actually exists, and so the courts can only be of help where an existing tort is committed. (A tort is a legal wrong, which does not have to be intentional but is defined by what is seen as people's general obligation to others.) Therefore you must look to see whether a tort has been committed or has been threatened. Torts include violence against you, interference with your property, trespassing on your property or causing any kind of physical harm or fear of harm to you.

Harassment from a former spouse or landlord Where there is no specific relationship between the harasser and the harassed (as above) it is more difficult to obtain an injunction. There may be no need to cause you any actual harm for it to constitute harassment, but for you to obtain an injunction, the harasser's behaviour must be seen by the court as intending to cause considerable inconvenience to you or your family.

Special provision, where the courts are less reluctant to grant injunctions, is made in two respects:

- harassment from a former spouse or common-law spouse
- harassment of a tenant by his or her landlord to get the tenant to move out.

When the person causing the problems is a former spouse or partner, who used to live with you or still lives with you, then it is easier to get an injunction to protect you from harassment and possibly to exclude him or her from your home. In serious cases the court can also order that he or she does not come within, say, 50 metres of the house. In this sort of case, the police become more involved and can arrest someone in breach of the injunction immediately if this power is attached to the injunction.

Tenants also have protection from harassment by their landlords. Where the landlord is trying to annoy the tenant so much that the tenant would feel forced to move out, for example by withholding a key to the premises, knocking holes in walls and ceilings, cutting off the water, gas or electricity, then the landlord is committing a criminal offence, and the tenant has the right to obtain an injunction. This is more effective in preserving the tenant's rights than pressing criminal charges against the landlord would be.

However, the landlord would have to be:

- breaching one or more of the terms of the lease (there is an automatic clause saying that the tenant has the right to quiet enjoyment of the property)
- trespassing on the tenant's home
- interfering with the tenant's personal property
- creating difficult circumstances for the tenant to live in.

Of course you are entitled to these injunctions in normal circumstances, but if it appears that the landlord is trying to persuade you to leave the property, then the court is more likely to order that he stops. *See* Chapter 5, Tenant's right to quiet enjoyment of the lease, page 94.

CHAPTER 3

Trouble with Your Neighbours

Here we are looking at situations where things happening off your premises cause you inconvenience or annoyance when you are at home, for example, noise or vibrations from building works next door that threaten your comfort and quiet enjoyment of your home. We also look at what happens when damage is caused or threatened to your property such as that from other people's pets or flooding from nearby.

A deliberate invasion of your property, such as someone dumping rubbish on your land, is automatically wrong according to the law, being a trespass (*see* The nature of trespass, page 31). Otherwise the law will look objectively at the problem and try to decide who is being unreasonable, you or your neighbour.

DAMAGE OR INCONVENIENCE

You need to distinguish between inconvenience and actual damage to your property.

For example, if children playing football next door kick a ball into your garden, there is a world of difference in what you can and should do when the ball merely lands on your lawn, or when it breaks one of the windows in your house or greenhouse. If an object that has been thrown or placed on your property has caused damage, *see* Damage caused to your property, page 62.

If no damage has been caused, there is little you can do, unless it is likely to happen frequently and be a constant nuisance. You have no right to keep the ball as a form of punishment or to stop the incident happening again, but if it happens regularly, then, failing any less confrontational methods, you may well be entitled to an injunction.

Summary

If you are unable to agree

- an injunction may be appropriate where you are inconvenienced or damage is threatened.
- you can claim compensation for damage if it occurs due to the acts of a neighbour or anyone else in the vicinity of your home.
- you can take positive action to sort out the problem yourself; this is called 'your right of abatement'.

INCONVENIENCE WITHOUT DAMAGE

What should you do when people allow or cause things like livestock or cars to come on to your property without permission?

Overhanging trees and branches

- You have the right to chop off the part of the branch that is on your side if the branches of a tree begin to grow over and on to your property, but only once it has actually grown on to your side, not before. The branch that you chop off still belongs to your neighbour, and so you must return it to him.
- You can also chop off the roots of any tree or plant that encroach on your property.
- You are entitled to chop off such a branch even when the council has placed a preservation order on the tree. However, only start attacking such trees if they are actually causing damage to your property.
- You are entitled to claim the cost of damage from an overhanging branch or root from your neighbour or whoever owns the tree, provided he knew that the branch concerned might damage your property in some way. This applies too when your neighbour really

---

Forbidden fruit

Any apples or other fruit that fall from an overhanging branch on to your property belong to the owner of the tree, rather than to you. A case in 1626 set the precedent which allows the owner of the tree to come on to your property to collect the apples.

---

ought to have known of the problem, even if he did not realise it or if his attention had not been brought to it.

Other invasion of your airspace

If something in your airspace is causing you inconvenience, then you may be able to get an injunction to stop it. You have a claim only when it interferes with the airspace that you actually need. For example a tower crane on a nearby building site which extends over into your airspace technically constitutes a trespass to your property. The court would be unlikely to award you an injunction unless this stops you from doing something you normally do or has caused any harm or damage. The court would recognise that the builders have a job to do, and that there may be no reasonable alternative but for the crane to come into your airspace.

A court would be unlikely to consider telephone wires going across your property to be such an inconvenience to you that it would order British Telecom to reroute them or replace them. The court has to look at the balance of convenience on both sides of any dispute.

Scotland There is an additional right known as 'stillicide' or 'eavesdrop', which states that your neighbour's drains may discharge rainwater on to your land, even if this causes you some inconvenience. However, if this is threatening or causing damage, such as water pouring down one of your walls, then your neighbour's right has gone too far and you are entitled to interdict.

Land encroaching on to yours

If your next-door neighbour extends his property on to yours, maybe by putting up a fence on your garden and then treating everything inside the fence as being his, then the property becomes his after 12 years (ten years in Scotland). This applies even where it was a previous owner who originally took over that part of your property, and the current owner then assumed that it was part of his property when he bought the house. This is because the 'twelve-year right' is attached to the land rather than the person. *See* Changing boundaries, page 23.

Straying livestock

A common problem in the countryside is sheep or cattle escaping from the field that they are kept in and coming into your garden. The owner will be liable for any damage caused or any expenses you incurred (within reason) while you were unable to return the livestock to him. The farmer's liability is irrespective of whether it was his fault or not, but if some of the fault can be put down to you then the compensation may be either reduced or completely wiped out.

Exceptions This does not apply either to livestock that stray from the road while the farmer is moving them from one field to another or for any other reason, or to animals kept on unfenced land, as is commonly the case in the north of England and Scotland.

Sometimes you will have the right to keep the animals in question – *see* Farm animals, page 77.

Dumping rubbish on your property

This is a criminal offence punishable with a maximum fine of £2,500 or three months in prison, or in theory both, but often you have no idea who is depositing rubbish on your property. Sometimes you can find out who is responsible by searching the rubbish for any details of their address, but there is little that you will be able to do. Your local council is obliged to take away your rubbish; for anything that is larger than normal, telephone them and ask them to remove it, providing that it is not completely inaccessible or impracticable to do so.

If you know who is responsible for the persistent rubbish dumping, and where they live, you may be able to get an injunction against them but your best remedy would be to report them to the police. You should be able to recover the cost of repair of any damage they have caused, but you will probably not get much compensation for the inconvenience.

Rubbish can cause you trouble even on your neighbour's property. For example where builders next door leave waste that blocks up your gutters or drains, you could claim compensation from the builders as the people who created the problem. In some cases you could recover compensation from either the builders or the neighbours.

Skips

If you need to hire a skip to deal with a lot of rubbish from your own home, and you need to keep the skip in the street, you have to get permission from your local council to put it there. The skip must be adequately lit so as not to cause a danger to traffic or pedestrians. The responsibility for this is usually shared between you and the skip hirers. Your council and/or the police may ask that the skip be removed or placed somewhere else.

Car parking

A constant source of frustration at home is the lack of space for car parking. What you can do about this depends on whether the parking is on the street (and therefore the responsibility of the council) or on your own property.

On the street Parking on the public street outside your house will normally be on a first-come-first-served basis. Since you have no defined right to park in any particular place, you also have no right to use dustbins or police cones to mark out your area until you return. This would constitute an obstruction of the highway, and you could be liable to a fine if you were caught. Where there is a permit system in operation, it is up to the local council to enforce the restrictions.

On other people's property You might have particular parking rights off your land that come with the property; check the deeds or the lease if you are unsure. Such a right can also arise if the area of the property has been used for parking for a long period of time (at least 20 years) with no problems. This area of law is extremely complicated though, since it has not yet been fully developed in the courts and such a right is unlikely to be shown in the deeds. If you are in any doubt you should consult a solicitor.

In front of your own property You do have some right to keep an area of the public street free for your access. However, other road users have a greater right to be able to use the road when they need to, so you cannot guarantee that no one will park in the way of your access. You could not threaten to clamp the cars of those who park there if it is not your own property.

If you believe that a car in your street or anything like an old shopping trolley has been abandoned, you should phone the local council and ask them to remove it.

On your own property If people are parking on your property without your permission then it is usually trespass. There is little you can do about this simple trespass that causes you no harm or damage. You cannot stop the owner returning to his car, unless he has actually caused damage (in which case you can only deprive him of his car until he has agreed to pay for the damage).

Example you would not be allowed to clamp his car unless you put a very prominent notice up on the wall where any driver could not really fail to see it, stating that a parking charge would be levied for anyone trying to park there.

If someone regularly parks on your property without your permission, then, failing all other solutions, you are entitled to seek an injunction against him.

> ### Return to sender
>
> If you write to the sender of the goods within 30 days of receiving the goods asking him to take them away, and the sender does not collect them within five months after that, then the 'unsolicited' goods become yours to keep for free.

Junk mail and unwanted goods

There is nothing you can legally do against advertisers putting junk mail through your letter box. You can sign up the Mailing Preference Service, which does its best to ensure that advertisers do not contact you by post. This is only likely to stop letters delivered by Royal Mail, and not flyers being posted through your door by private individuals.

Some advertisers distribute free sample goods which are normally yours to keep, but another form of junk mail is 'inertia selling'. You receive free goods, together with a letter saying that unless the goods are returned within a certain number of days then it is assumed that you have bought them. You are under no obligation to return them if you do not want to buy them, and it is the company who has to collect them in these circumstances.

Unless you want to buy it, you must not

- use or throw away whatever it is they are trying to sell you, since they might then be able to say that you have purchased it
- let it be damaged until it has been collected

NOISES, SMELLS AND GENERAL INCONVENIENCE

Interference with the use and enjoyment of your home caused by neighbours and nearby factories or shops is known in law as a 'nuisance'. It also covers an annoying event that occurs regularly.

Try to talk to the people responsible peacefully and rationally, and if that seems unsatisfactory try your local council.

When all else fails, you might be entitled to an injunction. It will have to appear that your neighbour is being unreasonable to other people living nearby, either by what he has done or by what he has failed to do. The law has to weigh up how annoying the problem would be to you (considering how serious the problem is and how long it has been going on for), against what your neighbour might be expected to do given his circumstances.

Powers of your local council

All councils are responsible for the control of anything that may affect the public health. They have the power to bring civil proceedings for the promotion or protection of the interests of people living in their area. This refers to

- sewers
- the prevention of diseases
- safety practices of local businesses and factories
- atmospheric pollution
- noise (wherever it comes from)

The council is concerned more with wider-ranging problems than disputes between neighbours. Since pollution and noise rarely affect only one person, your local council is the best place to go when things become difficult.

All these nuisances are known as 'statutory nuisances'. Local authorities are under a duty to serve an abatement notice when they believe that a statutory nuisance exists, ordering the person or people causing the nuisance to make sure that it stops. Things such as dust, smoke or foul gutters caused by local factories can possibly affect you; inform your council to take note of any such offence if they have not already done so. Noise can come from almost any source; many councils now have officials who regularly test the noise levels in certain areas.

The council can apply to the magistrates' or sheriff's court for a nuisance order if an abatement notice is disobeyed by those it is served upon. This has a similar effect to an injunction or an interdict.

Should this be disobeyed, those responsible will be liable to a fine. The amount is determined by the length of time that the problem continues (such as £50 per day); the longer the nuisance persists, the bigger the fine.

The council will usually be the most effective body to control problems like this. It is better than going to court for an injunction or an interdict.

Check Compare the councils' powers with those of the court (see below) before coming to a decision as to where to go.

Another relevant power of the council is planning control. For instance, a new factory might interfere with your TV reception, or block your view. If a new building nearby is going to seriously affect you, the council will carry out its own investigation.

You can object to planning application. The council can either reject the application for planning permission, or impose certain conditions upon it. See Chapter 6, Making Changes to Your Home.

Scotland There is a further right to claim damages where the nuisance was created by the neighbour purely out of spite for other neighbours, or a particular neighbour. This law is rarely used today, since most situations can now be covered by local authorities. It is presumed that people would prefer to get an injunction or interdict to stop the problem rather than receive damages for the inconvenience.

Powers of the courts

Where the problem is not 'public' enough, the council may not want to get involved and you will need to think of obtaining a court order. If the problem affects only you, you must consider whether that is because of any special circumstances that apply to you alone. The law is not prepared to accommodate any particular sensitivity you may have that others do not, whether this is due to what you do or to your own personal tolerance of problems. You might only have a case in law where the problem is particularly local or where the reason no others are affected is that you live in an isolated area.

You have to consider exactly against whom to get the injunction or interdict. Noisy pub-goers can create a problem for local residents when they leave, but you could not expect to identify them all in an injunction. Therefore your only option would be to get an order that the pub close earlier – an unlikely situation since there are very few areas in which a pub would be seen as unsuitable for the neighbourhood.

Some courts may also apply the old principle that it is only the actual owner, or the person in whose name the lease was made, who can actually bring an action in respect of his home.

The courts have always had power to restrain someone's activities or behaviour when they cause annoyance and inconvenience to neighbours, although your rights here are less straightforward than with trespass and damage. The 'activities or behaviour' can be

- making too much noise
- regularly burning fires so that the smoke constantly affects your property
- failing to ensure that their own property is maintained so that damage is caused or threatened to your property

The law looks at two main considerations:

1 Whether it is unreasonable, given where the problem is coming from and considering the practicalities of stopping the problem (is it inevitable?) and the character of the neighbourhood you live in

2 How long and to what extent the problem has been going on.

Examples It would be more difficult to stop a noisy factory from running a night shift if you lived on an industrial estate than if you lived in a residential area; or to stop your next-door neighbour's late-night parties if he only held three per year than if he held one a week.

If the problem is substantial (such as something preventing you from sleeping for most of the night), then only one or two occurrences of the problem will be enough for you to have the law on your side.

Action Keep a diary of any major disturbances.

Summary
The law is looking to find a fair balance between those who create the problem and those who have to suffer it – there is no automatic right to absolute peace and quiet. Demolition work has to be done, and is always going to be noisy and cause dirt and dust, but it should not be excessive.

The court will look to see what steps the demolition company and/or the property owner took to make sure that no undue inconvenience was caused to neighbours.

Think about how reasonable you are being. For example, if you work night shifts so that you have to sleep during the day, it would be unfair to expect everyone else in your area to stop doing things they would normally do during the day.

Follow the questions that the law asks and try to take an objective view, in order to put yourself in a better position to come to some arrangement with whoever is causing the problem. The time of day that it happens might be changed or you could take some action such as soundproofing in the case of excessive noise.

Beware Getting petitions together might only aggravate the situation.

Powers of the council compared with the courts

The powers of local councils to deal with statutory nuisance are increasing in scope and have become a far more effective and efficient way to control these sorts of problems than going to court.

- It is much cheaper. The council are under a duty to ensure that the nuisance is stopped, so they cannot charge you for the service.
- It is likely that the creator of the problem will pay more attention to the local council officials than to neighbours.
- The process is much quicker. However, the court system can be useful if it is a serious problem, and you wish to seek compensation for what you have had to endure.

Note You should only seek an injunction or compensation from the court in the severest circumstances. The court procedure for seeking injunctions is much more complicated than that for obtaining purely money judgements. Also as there is no special system for litigants-in-person, you may have to employ a solicitor to help you. (A litigant-in-person is someone who presents a case in court by themselves without representation by a lawyer.) (*See* Chapter 7, Resolving Disputes.)

If you do suffer damage to your property, or even personal illness, it may still be easiest to let the council stop the problem if it persists. You can then use the simpler methods for recovering compensation money through the courts if you cannot agree a compromise. Injunctions are best left to lawyers – whether or not you are entitled to legal aid, do everything possible to get the nuisance stopped another way.

Noise

Noise can have an almost infinite number of sources, such as next door's hi-fi, musical instruments or pets, a nearby factory's night shift, or a building site or workers in the street nearby.

Your local council has a duty to take action whenever it considers that the noise affects public health. It does not have to be something that causes injury, just something which interferes with personal comfort. The local council may adopt its own by-laws so the measures they may take will depend on the policy in your area.

The local authority's Environmental Health Department will deal with the trouble and have sophisticated noise measurement equipment. If they think the noise excessive amounting to a nuisance, they will serve an abatement notice on whoever is creating the problem, and bring the matter before the magistrates, or the sheriff if you live in Scotland.

The abatement notice will probably limit the amount of time the noise can be made, or possibly impose conditions, or specify changes which must be made by that person to the activity that causes the noise or seek to put a stop to the noisy activity altogether. The person has the right to appeal to the magistrates, or sheriff's court if he believes that it is unfair or puts an undue burden on him or his work.

You as a homeowner or tenant have the right to complain directly to the magistrates' court (or the sheriff's court). This can be easier than taking civil proceedings since you do not have to show that you have suffered interference; you must just show that the noise exceeds the levels set as the maximum for your area by the local Environmental Health Department. If the court is satisfied that the noise is excessive, it will make an order

---

False alarms

Some councils adopt a statutory code on burglar alarms so that only those that comply with certain requirements can be fitted in certain areas. They then have power to enter the premises (but not to use force to gain entry) to turn the alarm off after an hour. Unfortunately, no similar provision has been made yet in relation to car alarms.

---

similar to a noise abatement notice. (*See* Chapter 7, Resolving Disputes.) Your area may have been designated a 'noise abatement zone', that is a particular area in which noise should not be excessive. The council will monitor the noise coming from certain premises within the area which it believes to be excessive, and may take action without your being involved.

Local councils have special powers in relation to construction sites, demolition sites and road works and will often intervene when work is about to take place, imposing certain conditions such as times of working and levels of noise. However, they realise the work has to be done!

The law will not help you on noise created by traffic, by the armed forces, and by demonstrations, but generally the provisions apply to noise in the street as well as from neighbouring property.

Dangerous dogs

If there is a dangerous and apparently uncontrolled dog near your home this may be a council matter. It can be simpler, however, to make a complaint to the local magistrates' or sheriff's court, who can order the owner to either keep it under proper control, or have the dog neutered if it is male, or ultimately have the dog put down.

Pit bull terriers and Japanese tosa dogs now have to be muzzled if they are taken out in public, and it is illegal to breed or sell them.

Troublesome telephone calls and letters

See Harassment, page 44. 'Poison-pen letters' constitute a 'private' nuisance, so the council would be of no help to you. An injunction may be more appropriate if it really is necessary and if you know exactly who is causing the problem. In order to succeed, you would have to prove that it is that person to the court, and you will also have to know their address.

Vibrations

The same principles apply as in the problem of noise (*see* Noise, page 58).

Example A generator installed next door or building works going on in the vicinity of your property might create such bad vibrations in the foundations of your house that you find it difficult to sleep. It is possible that any such vibrations may threaten damage to your property. Your local council can help stop this, but you must act quickly since the damage can be extensive and fundamental to the structure of your house. An injunction from the court may be more appropriate in a very serious situation.

Smells

As with noise, the law will look at the balance of interests of the person creating the smell and the person(s) suffering. Much will go on the character of the area: if you live in an industrial area or on a street with many restaurants then the law states that you should expect some unfortunate smells. However, this is not a carte blanche for the factory or restaurant to do what it likes. There is still only a certain amount of nasty smells that they need to produce and exceeding this will mean that the council or court can stop them.

Nasty smells can also come from domestic premises. Neighbours attempting to pursue 'The Good Life', may be overstepping the mark in terms of smells from animals, manure and compost (and particularly the number of flies that might result). Genuine farms have much more freedom from control of the courts and the council, however, since many of the problems created for their neighbours are inevitable consequences of their activities.

Smoke and fumes

Everyone is entitled to light a barbecue or a bonfire in their garden throughout the year provided it is controlled and does not regularly cause a nuisance.

However, where a neighbour's fire or a nearby factory process is giving off smuts so that damage might be caused, the law will be on your side. If damage is actually caused then you can claim compensation; the money received will cover having to repaint the walls of your house if they are affected.

Commercial activities

You can object to planning permission or licences being given to new restaurants or pubs opening up nearby if you think that they may potentially create smells or noise. The restaurant may not be stopped from opening, but it will alert the council in order to make sure that it does not exceed what is necessary. The council or the magistrates might also impose some conditions on the way the restaurant operated if it felt that your fears were justified.

You might be entitled to an injunction, but only where the presence of such a commercial activity seriously threatens your enjoyment of your home.

The appearance of other people's houses

What other people do to their houses can be infuriating and can make you feel that your whole neighbourhood is degraded; unfortunately this is only a matter for the planning regulations in your area, (see Chapter 6, Making Changes to Your Home).

No sex please

In 1981 a group of residents successfully applied for an injunction against a sex shop that had opened up in a residential area of Pimlico in central London, because they said it might threaten the character of the area, and the values of their homes.

DAMAGE CAUSED TO YOUR PROPERTY

Deliberate damage

Deliberate damage to your property is normally a criminal offence. Hopefully you will be insured against the cost of the damage although usually you have to inform the police of the offence before the insurance company will deal with it. On a successful conviction for criminal damage, most courts will nowadays make a compensation order in favour of whoever suffered the damage or loss.

If you know who caused the damage then you can try to recover the cost by suing the perpetrator for the value of whatever was damaged or destroyed. You can take it to your local county court or sheriff's court if they refuse to pay you the money directly.

Unintentional damage which was somebody's fault

Compensation can normally be claimed against the person responsible provided that you can show all three of the following:

1 that they were at fault, either by doing something, or failing to do something when they should have
2 that what they did or failed to do caused the damage that you have suffered
3 that the damage you have suffered could have been predicted, given what they had done or failed to do.

If the person who caused the damage was trespassing on your property at the time you should be automatically entitled to compensation. The rules therefore only apply when the damage was less direct, such as your neighbour creating conditions next door which subsequently caused damage to your property.

Proving your neighbour was at fault

Your neighbours can be at fault even though they were doing something that they were perfectly entitled to do on or to their own property. If the neighbour's actions caused damage to your property or substantial inconvenience to you when they should have considered the consequences, it will be their fault. You must show that:

- What your neighbours did might have been a positive act. For instance, they might have constantly played music loudly, or allowed something to come on to your property which caused damage, such as a cricket ball breaking a pane of glass in your greenhouse.
- They might have been responsible for creating a state of affairs which then went on to cause problems for you. Perhaps they have resurfaced their drive with concrete, or allowed their drain to become blocked, either of which then causes water to overflow on to your premises. Any damage or inconvenience that your property suffers as a result of that overflowing water is their fault.

Often the damage is as a result of something your neighbours failed to do, when they knew, or ought to have known, that it was liable to cause damage to someone else's property.

Examples:
- failing to control the roots of a tree in their garden which then went on to damage the foundations to your house
- allowing damp to set in to their side of a party wall, and therefore damaging your side of it
- letting his dog damage your garden when they knew that it was likely to do so
- Allowing their gutters to block up or leak so that your property is flooded or the walls suffer water damage
- failing to control a bonfire, so that some of your property gets burned

Proving your neighbour caused the damage You need to show that there was a direct link between your neighbour's act or failure to act, and the damage to your property. This is usually self-evident.

Proving the damage was predictable You must show that the damage

---

Vive la France!

A quote from *The Times* of 6 February 1933: 'A Frenchman, in celebrating the restoration of Alsace to France in 1919, fired a revolver which burst and injured him. His claim that his injuries were due to the outbreak of war in 1914 was rejected by the Metz Pensions Board as too remote.'

---

you suffered was likely to happen because of what your neighbour did. You will need to consider precisely what damage you have suffered, and whether it was 'reasonably foreseeable' from the cause of the damage. This is to stop people claiming for peripheral items which are rather remotely linked with the substantive damage. It might be difficult if what was damaged was rather unusual in the context of the home.

- You may have difficulty claiming compensation for damage to something that is unusually delicate. So if your neighbour caused flooding which only killed some exotic and unusual plant in your garden the law might say that a lot of the fault was down to you (in the same way light or early sleepers might have difficulty preventing noisy parties from going on next door).

- You can only claim the difference between the money value of the damaged article before it was damaged and after. It is not as straightforward as just getting the cost of repair or replacement, since the law takes into account that it might have been several years old before it was damaged.

Pure accidents

Your insurance will cover situations when your neighbour was not at fault, or the damage was originally caused by something beyond his control. There are two exceptions where you can still claim compensation from your neighbour.

If your neighbour did nothing to create the problem themselves but ought to have contained it once it had happened to avoid further damage. Imagine that an unusually strong wind ripped their TV aerial from the roof so that it was hanging by the wire and was a potential danger to you or your property. If, several days later – during which time your neighbour ought to have fixed it – it fell off and damaged your property or injured someone, your neighbour would still be at fault.

If you live next door to factories or other commercial operations, the following might apply. Your neighbour may be storing something on their property in a way that is potentially liable to cause damage and is not a 'natural use'. If it comes from their property to yours, by whatever means and does cause damage, you are able to claim compensation. This does not apply in Scotland.

Example A chemical factory next door to your house which stored acid in a large tank would automatically have to compensate you for any damage done if that tank burst and the acid seeped on to your property.

'Non-natural use' is a wide-ranging field. Ask yourself if you would expect to find such a thing being kept in large quantities on property in your area. Past cases of 'non-natural use' have been
- water stored in large quantities (the amount you need for your home is considered 'natural')
- a large number of fireworks stored in a garage
- petrol in a car parked on the property.

Domestically 'non-natural use' might cover something like a weed-killer that your neighbour accidentally sprays over his fence, which then kills some of the plants in your garden or a container of bleach leaking and flowing towards your house so that your property is damaged.

What to do if you anticipate damage
A problem such as dry rot coming through to your house from your neighbour's house should be stopped as soon as possible, before any damage is done. The law allows you some solutions in the absence of mutual cooperation.

Here you have a 'right of abatement' which allows you to take action when your property is threatened with damage, even if it means going on to your neighbour's premises and interfering with his property. Compare also the possibility of getting a court order to allow you to go on to your neighbour's property to make repairs to your home when this is necessary, or your neighbour doing the same (*see* Neighbours carrying out repairs, page 38).

Note Be careful how you exercise this right of abatement. It does not allow you to do anything you want with your neighbour's property, only what is absolutely necessary to stop the problem. Let him know that you are going to do something about it (if he will not take any action himself) before you start to interfere with his property. However, in an emergency, you will be probably excused by the law for using your initiative.

It must be very clear that damage is going to be caused to your property if your neighbour carries out his plans.

For example, you might fear that subsidence will be caused if your neighbour builds a cellar near your property. Legally this may be mere speculation unless you obtain an expert's opinion.

You can obtain an injunction where damage may well occur if your neighbour does not stop something or allows something to happen. You are much more likely to get an injunction where there is a real threat of damage, rather than just inconvenience.

Where damage is threatened you are entitled to ignore the previous principles (*see* Noises, smells and general inconvenience, page 53) – namely looking at the character of the neighbourhood and the sort of activities that might be permitted there. But consider what effect an injunction would have on your neighbour, since it might stop him from doing essential work if there is no other way than to cause some damage. It might be that a court would just award you the cost of repair. Nevertheless, consider an injunction, if this be the only way to stop the problem.

The problem of subsidence

The actual land that you technically own as a freeholder (excluding the buildings on it) has a natural right of support, and you can get compensation if the land subsides due to the actions of somebody nearby, for instance mining works.

- You have no natural right which says that your property will be supported once additional weight (such as your house) has been added to the original soil, unless you can show, by the use of expert geologists and surveyors, that the subsidence would have happened even if your house had not been sitting on the land already.
- There is no right whatsoever against somebody who causes your land to subside by extracting the water underneath it, even if it would have happened whether there were buildings on it or not.

Exception Where the cause of the water drainage was a brine-pumping operation, the company must pay you compensation for the damage.

Where you think damage is threatened by subsidence due to somebody else's actions, you are entitled to an injunction, but you will have to show the court how it is that subsidence might occur. This will involve the use of expensive experts and comprehensive insurance may be your only hope here.

Scotland While landowners have only a natural right of support in respect of the land itself, (excluding buildings) a further right in respect of the buildings can develop. This occurs when the person who is causing the subsidence knows that there are buildings on your land that are at risk, or knew that buildings were likely to be erected on your land and might then be affected by any subsidence.

CHAPTER 4

Your Obligations as a Homeowner

Although your home is yours to enjoy as you wish, as a freeholder or leaseholder, legally you have certain obligations. These include the safety of all visitors to the home and responsibilities for pets and wild animals.

YOUR RESPONSIBILITY TO VISITORS

You are responsible for the safety of those you invite into your home including:

- friends
- salesmen
- those who are allowed into your home without your permission (*see* People who have a right to come on to your property, page 37) and people those visitors bring to your property
- builders and decorators

If someone were to injure themselves because of something dangerous in your home you would be responsible and might have to pay them compensation for that injury, known as 'damages'. If their property is damaged due to the state of your house or garden, you will be liable to pay compensation for that damage (*see* Recovery of money, page 131). This can extend to loss of earnings from work if it is a direct result of the injury, and so the amounts that are payable can be substantial.

Most household insurance policies cover your 'occupier's liability', but you should check any conditions on that insurance carefully.

Remember You can restrict your visitors to certain areas of the house or garden, and if they go outside those areas, then they are trespassing, and you will no longer be responsible for their safety. If there is a public footpath over your property then your responsibility will not extend to the condition of that footpath, since that should be the responsibility of the council, or the specific people who can use it.

Rented premises

On rented premises it is the tenant who is normally responsible for its safety, bar a few exceptions.

Landlords are responsible for any injuries sustained in the common parts of blocks of flats, and in other areas which they have a duty to repair. Visitors to your tenant in the flat that you rent out are not trespassing when they need to use the common parts of the property to get to it. You as a landlord would therefore have the obligation to ensure that those common parts are reasonably safe for anyone who might use them to get to the flats.

The tenant is responsible for the safety of the flat itself, provided that he genuinely has a full lease. It does not apply where he is only a lodger in part of your house or only has a licence (*see* What is a Tenancy or a Lease?, page 81). If the lease is for a period of less than seven years, or it states in the lease that the landlord is responsible for repairs (*see* Landlord's obligations to Repair, page 90), then the landlord is also responsible for

---

Danger!

Common dangers in the home include the following:

- loose pieces of carpet on which people might trip up
- poisonous plants in your house or garden which children might be tempted to eat
- slippery bathroom floors
- broken glass on the floor
- rickety banisters on staircases
- poorly stacked cupboards where the contents fall on whoever opens them

any injuries or damage sustained as a result of their failure to carry out the repairs. This applies to any repairs that must be made to the structure and exterior of the property, although it may also cover certain installations within the house or flat. This does not exempt the tenant from any liability as well, so any compensation may be shared if the tenant knew or ought to have known of the problem. This stems from the tenant's right to do the repairs himself and then charge the landlord for the cost.

When an accident is your fault

Your responsibility for accidents in the home depends on how much it is your fault, but this includes accidents which were the fault of somebody else you should have checked on.

You might be held responsible for any injury caused by faulty wiring installed by an unqualified electrician. You must ensure that he did the job competently, although no court would expect you to notice some obscure or minor defect. If it is done negligently then you should get it redone. If you employ a gardener who leaves a rake lying on the lawn and someone then treads on it, and injures him or herself, you are responsible for the accident.

- You will not be responsible for accidents which you could do little about or which were not as a result of your actions. Some activities are inherently dangerous, so you cannot prevent accidents happening. If you employ builders to alter the structure of your house, involving the demolition of interior walls, then, if a wall falls down and injures one of the builders, you will not be liable for his injuries.

- You will not be responsible for an accident if you believe it was the fault of the person injured. If they did not take care of themself when the danger was perfectly obvious, then no responsibility for any injuries should be yours. If, for example, they were drunk at the time and so fell into your swimming pool, it is likely to be entirely their fault.

The law might believe that both you as the householder and the injured person are responsible for the injury. For example, if someone has too much to drink at a party at your home and then falls off a balcony which ought to have had a railing on it, you might be considered 50 per cent

---

The Slippery Slope

Your obligation is to ensure, as reasonably practicable, that any visitors will be reasonably safe. So, for instance, if your path is icy in the morning and it is going to take a long time and a lot of salt to de-ice when you have to go to work, then you can leave the path as it is for the moment. (The postman should be aware that there may well be ice on your path anyway.) However, if it is only a short path and will only take a moment to sort out, then you should take care of the problem before anyone slips on it. Beware, though, that if you do attempt to de-ice your path, but do not do it properly, so that someone then slips on it, you will still be held responsible.

---

responsible for the accident. The court would award half the compensation that the injured person would be entitled to.

Warnings of the danger

You can abnegate the responsibility by warning visitors of the danger or potential problem, either orally or with a notice. It is no good, however, putting a tiny sticker next to the problem hoping that people will see it and understand it before anything happens. You need large, legible writing on a prominent notice which people can't miss.

Remember A notice will not be adequate for children, so you must take special care when they are on your property.

Once your visitor is fully aware of the risks it is up to them to be careful. But you must point out the dangers from the start. Putting up a notice should exclude your liability for any subsequent accident even if the person injured did not actually read the notice. The law is concerned with the lengths you went to, to make sure that your home was safe for people.

Responsibility to children in your home

If you have any children coming into your house or property you have a much greater responsibility to make sure that no danger will come their way. Be aware that children are liable to wander off, and will be attracted to anything that looks interesting (and may be dangerous). Poisonous berries in your garden, swimming pools and fish ponds, and many things in the kitchen and bathroom can be a danger to children.

Parents are expected to take a certain amount of responsibility for overseeing their children, especially if they are very young. But in the end the person responsible for any injury caused by the state of your home will normally be you. A notice or warning to a child on your premises will have little effect since a court would not expect the child to be able to read or take in the full meaning of the warning, although this will depend on the child's maturity. If the child's parents are present then the warning should be given to them as well. For example, a small child plays on some banisters that are marginally too wide to stop him falling through. One might expect both the owner of the house and the parent of the child to share equal responsibility for the child's actions.

There is no specific age of awareness of danger in children; you must judge what the child in question may do, depending on his age and development. You should make sure that you know where they are at all times, and be aware of anything that might fascinate them or be a tempting thing to play with.

Another important exception is your possible liability for any injuries they sustain even when they are technically trespassing on your property. This would apply only where it would be likely that children would trespass there, or where you already knew that children trespassed there. Therefore you should take all precautions possible when you have something potentially dangerous on your property that children might not be able to resist. This could be a disused property of yours or building works on your premises. Make sure that it is boarded up and as child-proof as possible. Sometimes they will get in whatever you do, but if the court decides that you have not done all you really can (within reasonable expense) then you will still be liable for any injuries they sustain.

Summary

1 You can be liable for any injuries that children sustain due to the state of your land, even when they are trespassing.
2 Whether trespassing or not, you have to be far more careful about what might happen to children since they cannot be expected to look after themselves like an adult can.
3 The option of warning visitors rarely applies to children, especially written warning, since the courts will not normally expect the child to be able to read it.

YOUR RESPONSIBILITY FOR ROAD USERS' ACCIDENTS OUTSIDE YOUR HOUSE

The rules are stricter than above because whoever is injured does not have to establish that the injury was actually your fault, in that you might not have known or have been expected to know about the problem. However, you are only responsible for the parts of the property that you own or rent, and not for the condition of the pavement itself, unless it is privately owned by you.

- You must make sure, if your house is on a street, that no potential danger arises to people on the road or pavement because of such things as a dilapidated wall or loose slates. Consider things such as window boxes which might be blown off, and loose tiles on the roof; these are potential hazards to passers-by or people calling at your house, such as the postman or the milkman.
- You will be liable for any damage or injury even if it was your builder's fault. However, where the danger results from an unusually high wind or something beyond your control then you will incur no liability.
- If you rent the house or flat concerned, your landlord may be responsible for any necessary repairs to the outside of the house, including the parts of it that border the road. Where a lease is for less than seven years the landlord is automatically responsible for these

repairs. But you must still take care to see that there are no dangers to road-users, since it will be both you and your landlord who are liable for any compensation. You can get the repairs done yourself and then charge your landlord for the expense. (*See* Landlord's obligations to repair, page 90.)

Possible compensation following accidents

Compensation for property damage or injuries is known as 'damages'. The court will award damages to cover the cost of either repairing or replacing the damaged property (whichever is cheaper), or a sum of money that represents the pain and severity of the injury that was sustained, given the circumstances of the injured person.

In British courts you cannot get damages for just about any conceivable loss that might come out of an injury or damage to property. People can only recover damages for actual financial loss where it was their injury or damage that caused that loss. If a businessman is injured on your premises and has to take time off work, it may be very difficult for him to show that his time off was directly linked to any loss of profits of his business. Matters such as these will be dealt with by the insurance company that provides your household insurance, since most insert a clause which indemnifies you in the event of accidents on your property.

PETS AND OTHER ANIMALS

There are special rules which relate to animals, and which apply whether the damage or injury they cause takes place on or off your property.

Dogs
- All dogs must wear a collar (with your name and address on it) when in a public place and should be kept under proper control.
- Some places have their own rules or by-laws which state that dogs must be kept on leads.
- As with noisy neighbours, a noisy dog which barks all night can give rise to the service of a noise abatement notice.

If the owner deliberately sent the dog on to your property, it constitutes a trespass and you are entitled to ask that he remove the dog. Failing this, you can remove the dog from your premises yourself.

If the dog or cat comes on to your property while its owner is not looking, it is only when this is a regular occurrence and is a serious annoyance or when it actually causes some damage, that you have an action in law.

Pets are unpredictable, but if you have a pet which you know might cause serious damage or injury you will normally be liable for any accidents that do happen, whether your fault or not. For example, while Jack Russells are normally fairly placid creatures, they are known to be aggressive and may bite humans, particularly at meal-times. Most pets come into this category, although cats have been excluded in past cases, as it appears that they are never expected to cause injury or damage.

If your dog, which is always very friendly but sometimes becomes rather aggressive towards strangers on your property, suddenly bites the postman, you will be liable to him for compensation. If, however, the dog had never bitten or shown aggression to anyone before (which is generally unlikely when looked at objectively), then you would not be so liable.

If you live near a farm, you must make sure that your dog does not escape and injure any livestock, otherwise you will have to pay compensation to the owner. This may include game birds, which are often vulnerable, although the rule does not apply if the farmer's animals have strayed on to your property. Ultimately the farmer is entitled to kill your dog if he believes that it is worrying his animals.

You are not liable for damage or injury where you have taken all precautions possible or it is entirely the fault of the victim (as in your general responsibility for dangers to visitors to your home). You may also escape liability when the victim is a trespasser on your property, although not when you keep your dog more as a guard dog than a pet.

Wild animals on your property

Protected animals and birds remain protected even when they are on your property and causing a nuisance, whether in the house or garden.

Protected animals

These animals are protected by law: badgers, bats, rainbow leaf beetle, field and mole crickets, Norfolk aeshna dragonfly, wart-biter grasshopper, sand lizard, great crested newt, otters, smooth snake, fen raft spider, ladybird spider, red squirrel and natterjack toad.

In addition the following snails, butterflies and moths are protected:

Snails:	carthusian, glutinous, sandbowl
Butterflies:	chequered skipper, heath fritillary, large blue and swallowtail
Moths:	barberry carpet, black-veined, Essex emerald, New Forest burnet, reddish buff

For example, if bats or any of the other animals listed below choose to set up home in your attic, there is little that you can do about it. You are committing a criminal offence by: killing or injuring them, damaging or destroying where they live, even obstructing their access to wherever they live. You are committing a crime just by disturbing them in their habitat.

All wild birds and their nests and their eggs are protected, except game birds when they are in season.

Farm animals

If you live near a farm and livestock stray into your garden and causing extensive damage, the farmer will normally be liable for the cost. However he will not be liable for the damage or inconvenience if you do not have adequate fencing around your property. He would also not be liable if livestock escape on to your land while being moved on the road.

You actually have the right to detain the animals that have strayed on to your property, as long as you let the owner know within 48 hours that you have detained them. You must return them when requested, unless they have caused damage, when you must return them as soon as the farmer or owner has offered to pay the compensation you are entitled to. If no one comes to get them after 14 days, you have the right to sell (but

YOUR OBLIGATIONS AS A HOMEOWNER 77

not to kill) the animals, but you will have to pay back any excess over any damage or expenses if the farmer later comes to claim them back.

YOUR LOCAL COUNCIL AND YOUR HOME

Your local authority can enter your home for inspection relating to matters such as planning and public health – for example, the drainage system to your house. After inspection the council may serve notice that certain works need to be carried out by you for your home to meet public health standards. These require work to be undertaken if the premises are likely to cause injury, damage health in any way, or adversely affect the comfort and quality of life of particular people.

If you are a leaseholder paying full rent to your landlord regularly on a lease that was originally for less than seven years, it will be up to him to ensure that the works are carried out. However, if you bought a long-term lease and pay only a nominal ground rent, it will usually be up to you. If the council serve a notice on you, they should be able to advise who is responsible for carrying out the works.

Council duties and powers

The council have a duty to take away your household rubbish but they might impose by-laws in order to make the job easier. For instance, you are always required to keep the access to your dustbins clear so that the dustmen can get to them.

Some local authorities will only take rubbish put in particular dustbins, and they have the power to do this. However, if you wish to challenge this, you are entitled to appeal to your local magistrates' court. It will decide the matter provided you appeal within 21 days of the council informing you of their new requirement.

The council are responsible for the sewerage to your home, the cleaning of the streets, and many other aspects of public health and cleanliness; for some of these purposes its inspectors and officers have the right to enter your home. The council have similar responsibilities for dilapidated properties which have fallen into a serious state of disrepair as a result of neglect by the owner.

Councils retain the powers to regulate the development of the area. The district or borough council regulates not only what is developed and how property is used, but also how any building work or structural changes are carried out to your property (*see* Chapter 6, Making Changes to your Home).

Councils can impose preservation orders on trees on your land. After a preservation order it becomes an offence for anyone, including the landowner (the owner of the tree), to chop down or otherwise harm the tree. There is no liability if the tree falls down of its own accord, as long as you did nothing that might have caused this.

Council tax

Council tax charges by the 'dwelling' rather than by the number of people over the age of 18 living in it. The amount you pay is determined by the value of your property and the council will have put you in one of eight bands, A to H. The person normally responsible for paying council tax is the person who lives in the house, (whether owned or rented).

If your house is a family home you and your spouse will be jointly liable for council tax. Lodgers and those renting a flat within your house are liable for their own proportion of the tax, although an arrangement may have been made with the landlord regarding the payment.

Making a clean (chimney) breast of it

Whether you are allowed to light a fire in a fireplace in your home depends on whether you are in a 'smoke control area' as decided by your local council. It was decided in the 1950s that the smog in some cities was too much and some controls had to be laid down. You can find out whether your home is within a smoke control area by telephoning your council, although the restrictions usually only apply in urban areas. The council might not necessarily impose a total ban on the use of chimney fires, but they might stipulate the use of a certain type of coal or the design of the fireplace or chimney. Failing to follow the regulations for your area may render you liable to pay a fine, after one warning from the council.

Exception You may be 'flat-sharing' with others who are not members of your family. Where two or more people who are not related have their own bedrooms but share the kitchen, bathroom and living room, it is only the owner who is liable to pay council tax. However, co-habitants will be treated as a married couple and are both liable to pay the tax.

Appeals If you believe you are not liable to pay but have been charged, or if you disagree with the value that the council have put on your property, you are entitled to appeal to your local valuation tribunal but only

- When you have reached an impasse with your council. You must be seen to have tried to solve the problem with your council, for example by writing a clear letter to the council that sets out your grievance.
- If they do not reply to your letter within two months
- If the council dismisses your grievance or says that it is dealing with the problem even though nothing has happened.

Scotland The owner of a property may have to pay feuduty to a superior. It only applies to properties that have not changed hands since 1974, since all feuduties now have to be redeemed upon sale.

MORTGAGE OBLIGATIONS

Most houses today are purchased by way of a mortgage, *see Good Housekeeping Consumer Guide: Buying and Selling Your Home* (Ebury Press, £6.99), but you should be aware that mortgages bring obligations. Most of these are contained in the mortgage deed that you agreed with the bank or building society which lent you the money. They concern

- paying instalments on the mortgage
- insuring the property and keeping it in a good state of repair, and
- letting the lender know of anything which might affect the value of the property, including any changes such as altering the structure or letting the property out to tenants.

Remember Your home is the bank's or building society's security for the money they lent you. Technically a mortgage entitles the lender to take possession and run the property as soon as you have signed the mortgage agreement, but all mortgages in practice say that the lender will not do this unless one of the conditions of the mortgage is breached. The only condition of relevance to this is repaying the instalments and interest. Many lenders require that they give their consent before you make a decision to let out your property; this would be specifically mentioned in your mortgage deed.

Falling behind on repayments

If you do fall behind on mortgage repayments, the bank or building society has the right to take possession proceedings if it fears that you may default further. When the mortgage is in respect of a residence rather than a business it is not entitled to take possession without a court order; the courts are reluctant to do this when they believe that you will be able to make good your default and any arrears. The court will adjourn the proceedings to a future date to allow you to comply with a new arrangement for payment of the instalments and any arrears.

Remember Set out the ways that you think you have of showing the court and the lender that you will be able to catch up again in the near future. This will involve going to court (there should be little need for a solicitor) and appearing before a district judge with the representative from the bank or building society. Usually only after repeated failures to pay the instalments, and the failure of the bank to believe that you are in a position to make good your default will the court actually make the necessary order for repossession.

CHAPTER 5

Letting Your Home and Tenants' Rights

WHAT IS A TENANCY OR A LEASE?

The right of the tenant to live in what is ultimately someone else's property depends on the consent or agreement of the landlord at the start. (N.B. To simplify matters, 'he' is used when refering to a landlord or tenant.)

Tenancies

These are periodic lettings, where the premises are let from week to week or month to month until it is terminated by the landlord. A tenancy might arise just from the weekly or monthly acceptance of a rent cheque.

Leases

These are for a particular period, fixed from the start, although there may be a right to renew the lease when it expires. Thus there is no need for any written agreement between the landlord and the tenant for there to be a lease or a tenancy (unless the lease is for three years or more). Tenancies and leases are virtually the same thing in this book as they both give the tenant that all-important 'right in the property'.

Licences

These give the tenant a right to occupy premises where the landlord has given permission to the tenant to reside on his property rather than a right in the property itself. The tenant – known here as a 'licensee' – does not 'hold' the property (*see* Leaseholders/tenants, page 14). The landlord can ask a tenant to leave the premises whenever he wants, although he might be in breach of contract and have to pay the tenant damages if required to leave before an agreed time. And because the licensee has no right 'in the property', their right cannot be enforced against any future landlords.

Licences give very few rights to the 'licensee' to stay on the property, so it is important to know when licences arise as opposed to leases.

Ask yourself the following:

- Do you have what is known as 'exclusive possession' of the property or area that you live in? If the landlord has the right to come into all parts of the property whenever he wishes, whether for cleaning for your benefit, or just for their own use, then you do have a licence not a lease. You need a part of the house, such as your bedroom, which no one else has a right to enter, for you to have a lease or a tenancy. This exclusive possession has to be conferred on you by the landlord.

- Is your right to reside in the premises for a certain period of time? This is a necessity for a lease or a tenancy. If you rent your home by the week or month then this will do, even though you do not know in which week the landlord might ask you to leave; you will only be required to leave at the end of the current week or month. With a lease you are granted the right to reside there for a fixed period of time, and you know precisely when that time is. It would not be a fixed period of time if you were allowed to live there until 'the landlord needed the premises for someone else' since no one can tell exactly when that might be.

With a licence, you have little security as regards your right to remain on

---

Flat-share

Where a landlord grants tenancies to people sharing a house, it should be decided then who is to have which room, rather than leaving this to be decided between the flat-sharers otherwise they will only have a licence rather than a lease.

the property. As a tenant under a tenancy or lease, you actually have a legal interest in the land. You own the right to live there, and can treat the land as your own for the time being, even selling that right to live there (subject to any restrictive clauses in the lease or tenancy agreement).

Pros and cons

A lease gives you protection from what your landlord might do, such as selling the property while you are still living there. As a tenant you are allowed to stay there until the tenancy is ended or the lease expires, even when ownership of the freehold changes hands – the new owner has only bought the right to hold the property once your right finishes.

As a licensee your right to stay there comes from the landlord alone, so if there is a new landlord he is entitled to withdraw that permission. However, licensees are normally entitled to protection from eviction, and have the same rights to enjoy the property as tenants.

Note In some cases a person under a licence has been able to enforce their rights for a longer period than the landlord originally intended. A landlord might say to someone, 'You are entitled to stay here as long as you wish.' This is not a lease, just a licence as a defence to trespass. Legally the landlord can withdraw that permission whenever he likes, unless the person he invited to stay has done something for his own benefit on reliance of that original promise, such as build somewhere to live on the landlord's property. This is the law's way of making sure that people stick to their promises and where people have spent money in reliance on that promise, it will protect them. Ask a solicitor to clarify just how much right the licensee has to stay on the property.

Scotland The concept of licence barely exists, and a tenant will have a proper tenancy or lease so long as the tenant pays rent to the landlord by agreement, and there is a fixed date when the lease will come to an end. Leases will still not arise where there are:

• resident landlords
• holiday lettings
• shared-ownership agreements.

Granting the lease

Tenants need to be very careful about the stipulations that are made when your landlord grants you your lease. ('Lease' will now mean either a tenancy or a lease since there is no longer any need to distinguish them.) Leases are normally contained in a document which outlines precisely what you can and cannot do.

Remember Because the document calls itself a lease, it does not automatically mean that you have a lease – whether it is a licence or a lease depends only on those two factors above. If the lease is originally made for three years or more (not counting any right to renew the lease) in England and Wales, or one year in Scotland, then it must be in the form of a signed document to be a proper lease.

Kinds of leases

Different kinds of leases are determined by
* whether the tenant will gain 'security of tenure' (the right to stay in the property even after the lease has expired)
* whether the tenant can have the level of rent scaled down by an independent rent committee.

Most tenancies created on or after 15 January 1989 (when the 1988 Housing Act came into force) are either assured tenancies or assured shorthold tenancies, Later we will look at what happens where the landlord resides at the same property as the tenant – a different situation.

Note None of the considerations below apply to licences. Whether the licensee has the right to remain at any time is a matter for the landlord, subject to the laws of contract.

Scotland Similar provisions apply, although the assured shorthold tenancy is known as a 'short assured tenancy'. The Housing (Scotland) Act 1988 came into force on 2 January 1989; assured tenancies, whether short or otherwise, can exist from that date.

Assured shorthold tenancies

This form of tenancy gives the tenant no right to remain in the property once the lease has expired.

- It must be for a fixed term, which must not be less than six months.
- The landlord must give the tenant a prescribed form of notice before granting the tenancy, telling the tenant that they have limited security of tenure.
- The tenant has the right to refer the rent to a rent assessment committee for its consideration.
- The landlord has no right to end the tenancy before the end of the first six months.
- The tenant has no right to terminate during this period, unless there is a clause in the lease which specifically entitles him to do so.

Failure to give the tenant a Notice of Assured Shorthold Tenancy before the lease is granted will mean that an assured tenancy is created and the landlord loses all the advantages of the tenant having no security of tenure.

The courts have no power to ignore either a failure to do this, or even a defect in the procedure, and so an assured tenancy will arise.

Check the Notice is in the form the law says it should be at the time the landlord grants the lease. Buy a current Notice from a legal stationer.

Any time during the assured shorthold tenancy (not once the fixed term has come to an end and the tenant resides under a different kind of tenancy) the tenant may refer the rent to the local rent assessment committee who will determine the maximum that the landlord may charge for rent during the entire tenancy. The committee will compare the rent to similar properties in the area, and declare a maximum, which will then be automatically incorporated into the lease. They look for a reasonable rent on the open market, rather than the old 'fair rent' system which took the rent below the market value.

The assured shorthold tenancy has become the most popular form of private letting for landlords, since it offers so few rights of security of tenure to the tenant. The landlord knows that he can grant a tenancy for a fixed period of time. Provided he uses the correct Notice and serves it on the tenant before the lease is made, he can guarantee that either he can expect the tenant to leave or he can evict him at the end of the lease, without having to prove any of the statutory grounds of possession as with the other kinds of lease.

Assured tenancies

Assured tenancies arise when the requirements relating to shorthold tenancies are not complied with, where the lease was created after 15 January 1989.

The difference is that once the lease has expired, the tenant has the right to stay on in the property unless the landlord can show one of the prescribed 'grounds for possession'. This may end up in court since some of the grounds for possession are 'mandatory' (so that the landlord automatically has the right to repossess the property), whereas some are 'discretionary' (so that it is for the court to decide whether it is reasonable for the landlord to regain possession) (see Other grounds for possession, page 99).

The rent under these tenancies may not be referred to a rent assessment committee, and market forces alone determine the level of rent. It can be complicated, however, for a landlord to increase the rent while the lease is running unless there is specific provision contained in the lease for this.

Rent Act tenancies

Tenancies created under the Rent Act 1977 are mostly those which were made before 15 January 1989. They give the tenant both substantial security of tenure and the means to get a rent which is lower than the market value for the property concerned. These advantages to tenants gave rise to the Housing Act 1988 assured tenancies and assured shorthold tenancies, since it was found that landlords were so reluctant to let their properties that there simply were not enough rentable properties to go round.

Different mandatory and discretionary grounds for possession apply in these cases, (see pages 101-2) although Rent Act tenancies are now diminishing in number.

At any time during one of these tenancies, the tenant may apply to the rent officer at his local council to have a 'fair rent' registered in respect of the property. The only way the landlord can set a rent higher than this is to apply for his own registration of a higher fair rent, and he must serve notice on the tenant that the rent will be increased before he can introduce the higher charge.

Resident landlords in the property

Where the landlord lives with the tenants in the same property, there is a legal exception to the forms of leases producing an assured tenancy.

No security of tenure arises in these circumstances. It is consequently easier to evict a tenant once the fixed term of the lease has expired or a notice to quit has been served on a tenant under a tenancy.

To qualify for this exception
- the landlord must be resident throughout the whole of the tenancy, although they are obviously allowed to take holidays and may sell the property during the term of the tenancy so that another landlord takes his place.
- The landlord must be resident from the start of the tenancy, so that this provision will apply to lodgers (where the tenancy is not a licence), flat-sharing with the owner of the flat, and au-pairs and nannies living in their employer's house.

Resident landlord

Slight complications arise when there is a self-contained flat that is part of the landlord's house, or where the landlord converts a large house into several flats which he rents out but retains one of them to live in. Thus if the house was originally built as flats then an assured shorthold tenancy may arise. If, however, the house was converted into flats from the original single house then the landlord will still be seen as a resident landlord.

Holiday lettings

No assured tenancy will arise where the house or flat is let for the purpose of a holiday let. The law looks objectively at the intentions of the 'landlord and tenant' before the letting was agreed to see whether this was indeed the purpose.

Long-term leases

Many flats, particularly in London, are bought on a long leasehold rather than freehold, often as a matter of convenience for the landlord since it can be difficult to delineate the boundaries of flats from the land they are supposed to own the freehold in. (The transfer of land upon sale relates to the actual land rather than the house that happens to be attached to it.)

Having a long leasehold, such as 99 years, is rather like buying a freehold for a number of years but paying a nominal rent each year to the landlord. The landlord has few obligations regarding repairs and maintenance if the lease that is granted is for more than seven years.

The tenant is able to buy the freehold in the flat or extend the lease for a further period of time without the landlord's consent. This is your 'right to buy' where the original lease was granted for longer than 21 years. Many flat-owners now choose to exercise the right to club together and buy the freehold of the block of flats that they live in.

Subtenancies

A tenant technically owns the right to live in the house or flat he rents and in respect of which he has a lease (not a licence). He is entitled to sell this right on to someone else, unless this is expressly forbidden in the lease. He can only sublet for a shorter period than his own tenancy but, in general, any of the above leases can exist in the same way between a tenant and a subtenant. As long as the subtenancy was not granted in breach of a clause of the original 'head' lease, then the subtenant also has the right to live in the house with both the landlord and the original tenant.

Council tenancies

Local councils which grant tenancies in their properties cannot grant assured tenancies or assured shorthold tenancies. They normally grant 'secure tenancies', which give the tenant a great deal of security of tenure. The only way they can be ended is by a court order.

There are many terms that are automatically implied in council tenancy leases, particularly regarding
- improvements to the property
- subletting the property (although you are allowed to take in lodgers).

Council tenants also have the right to buy their house, or a 125-year lease in the case of flats. They can get a substantial discount provided they have lived in council accommodation for at least two years. Contact your local council if you want to buy your council house.

Housing associations

These operate similar leases to those already described above, depending on whether they are privately owned or council-owned. You may therefore have either an assured tenancy, an assured shorthold tenancy, or a secure tenancy, or a Rent Act tenancy if the lease was granted before 15 January 1989.

RIGHTS AND OBLIGATIONS OF LANDLORDS AND TENANTS

The lease

The lease document outlines most of the rights and obligations between the two parties to a tenancy or lease. The document works in much the same way as a contract except that the obligations can pass from one person to another.
- If the landlord sold the property on to another buyer, then the buyer would inherit the rights and obligations that were first agreed (*see* Freeholds and leaseholds, page 11).
- If the tenant sublet (assuming that the lease allows him to do so), the subtenant has to accept all the terms of the lease that the original tenant agreed to.

- Breaching the terms of the lease may give rise to injunctive proceedings in the courts in the case of obligations, or repossession of the property by the landlord. The tenant might even be able to withhold some of the rent in respect of what the landlord's failure to carry out any of his obligations has cost him.

Note It is always wise to have a properly drawn-up lease outlining the precise obligations and rights that the landlord or tenants require. However, the law automatically places many other obligations and rights into all leases even when they are not actually mentioned. Some can be excluded if desired, such as the tenant's right to sublet the property to another person during his tenancy. Some may not be excluded in any circumstances, such as the landlord's obligation to maintain and repair the structure of the building when the lease is for less than seven years.

We will look at these 'invisible' rights not normally included in leases, because they apply to all leases provided the correct conditions are fulfilled.

Landlord's obligations to repair

This is often inserted in a lease or tenancy agreement, but the law states that there are always particular obligations in specified circumstances. These only concern 'repairs' rather than 'improvements' to the house or flat; the landlord is not expected to install something new to solve a problem in the house.

Parliament has decreed that for all tenancies which were originally granted for less than seven years (even if the tenant has subsequently been there for more than seven years) the landlord has to keep the following in good repair and proper working order:

- The structure and exterior of the house. This means the walls and foundations of the house, so the landlord will be responsible for things like repointing the walls. It also covers the repair of drains, gutters and external pipes attached to the property. However, the

tenant is obliged to make sure that they do not become blocked as a
day-to-day part of running the house. This is part of the tenant's duty
to 'act in a tenant-like manner'.

- The installations in the house for the supply of water, gas and
  electricity, for heating the house and heating water, and for sanitation
  (including basins, sinks, baths and sanitary conveniences, but not
  other fixtures, fittings, and appliances for making use of the supply of
  water, gas or electricity). There is no obligation on the landlord to
  improve the property, so that if the house does not have these to start
  with, he does not have to install them.

A landlord always has the right to enter the rented property in order to
carry out these repairs and to inspect the condition of the property.
Normally under a lease he has no such right to enter the property since the
tenant has exclusive possession of the property.

Whenever anything needs to be repaired, the tenant should inform the
landlord. The obligation to repair only arises when the landlord knows
about it, and that it is definately in need of repair (or where it is so obvious
that he really ought to have known).

If the landlord does not keep to these obligations despite being told
then the tenant is entitled to have the necessary work carried out himself
and recover the cost from the landlord. The tenant must be sure that the
repairs are in a class that the landlord is liable for. The tenant can withhold
rent to recover the cost of the repairs if it is in this class.

The premises may be in such a state as to constitute a statutory
nuisance, and so the council can deal with the landlord themselves by
serving an abatement notice on the landlord.

Tenant's right to a habitable property

Legally a house or flat does not have to be in a fit and habitable state at all
times for a tenant to live in, apart from some limited circumstances when
this is automatically a condition of the lease. This will usually only arise at
the beginning of the lease, where a tenant may be about to move into an
uninhabitable house and the landlord says that he will make the house

---

Landlord's liability for some accidents

When the landlord has the obligation to repair the property and knows or ought to have known of any repairs that are needed, he is liable for any damage or injury to anyone else caused by the adverse condition of the property. The liability does not fall on the tenant alone (*see* Chapter 4, Your Obligations as a Homeowner). The tenant must let the landlord know of any defects in the property since the landlord is liable for an injury as well as the tenant. The tenant may also contact the Environmental Health Department at his local council since the condition of the building may constitute a threat to public health.

---

habitable before the tenant does actually move in. Here the tenant is entitled to refuse to take up the lease if the landlord does not keep to this promise. The same would apply to a brand new house that has just been built, but for which the lease was agreed before completion of the building and decoration.

However, there need be no such prior agreement when the landlord is letting a furnished property. In this case if the house or flat is not in a fit condition for human habitation at the beginning of the tenancy, then the tenant can go back on the agreement and refuse to take up the lease.

Tenant's obligations

The tenant must repair the property as part of the day-to-day running of the house, such as unblocking drains and refitting loose carpets. This and most other similar obligations of the tenant are contained in the lease.

Health risk

The local council has powers to order the owner of a building to clean and disinfect premises that are considered a threat to public health, whether the property is furnished or unfurnished.

Common parts of the property

The landlord will normally retain control and occupation of the common parts of a property. This may include a staircase in a block of flats, even though the tenants in the flats have a right of way up the staircase if they need to use it to get to their flats. He is responsible for the repair, decoration and maintenance of the staircase, and is liable for any accidents that happen to people who are entitled to be on them, when that accident was the landlord's fault.

Tenant's right to buy

This applies to people who have 'bought' a long leasehold and pay only a nominal 'ground rent' each year, where the lease was for 21 years or more, and where they have lived in the property for at least three years in the case of buying a new lease, and one year in the case of buying the freehold.

The new rules as from 1993 allow the freeholds or leaseholds of virtually all residential houses and flats to be bought.

You need to serve on the landlord a notice of desire to purchase the freehold or extended lease, and then agree a price with the landlord. You should be paying the market value for the freehold, which can be set by an independent chartered surveyor. If the landlord refuses to agree to the price suggested, then you are entitled to appeal to the leasehold valuation tribunal.

Flats

The practicalities of buying freeholds in a block of flats are more complex because you cannot buy the freehold for the individual flat.

The tenants in the block must club together to buy the freehold of the entire block or structure within which the flats are contained. The rules now provide that a minimum of two-thirds of the residences in the block need to be willing to buy the freehold for the right to be exercisable. Other conditions are that the lease was originally granted for over 21 years and the tenant has used the flat as his main home for the last year, or a total of three years out of the last ten; these other conditions have to be fulfilled by at least half of the tenants in the block.

The same procedure as for buying houses applies here. However, there may be problems as to the actual ownership of the freehold. In English law no more than four people can own any one property, and so it may be easiest to set up a limited company which all the flat-owners in the block have shares in. A management committee made up from the shareholders can then become directors so that obligations regarding the building that usually fall on the landlord can be dealt with by them.

There is no automatic right for tenants to extend their lease or buy the freehold if they do not come within the statutory qualifications (see above). Such a right might be inserted into the lease at the start of the tenancy, however, stipulating the price and term of years. The tenant may then act upon it according to any conditions specified in the clause.

Tenant's right to quiet enjoyment of the lease

After a lease has been granted the landlord can do little to remove the tenant unless the tenant breaches the clauses of the lease or the landlord has another ground for possession (unless it is an assured shorthold tenancy). Unless the tenant is cooperative and also wishes to move out of the property, court proceedings are the only way. The rules that govern the recovery of property by a landlord against a tenant apply to all leases (*see* Recovering Possession of the Property, page 95).

Tenants have an automatic right to quiet enjoyment of the property, and this clause is often inserted in written leases.

It is a criminal offence for the landlord to attempt to evict a tenant
- by harassing him
- or trying to make the tenant's life difficult by controlling some of the premises upon which the lease operates.

Cutting off the tenant's electricity will amount to a crime where the court believes the motive was to persuade the tenant to give up his right to occupy the premises when the landlord wanted it back.

This is all very well as a deterrent to landlords or their heavies but it does not solve the problem from the tenant's point of view; they have lost their home, or may be enduring miserable circumstances. The criminal law system can be slow, and the prosecution has to prove the case to a much higher standard than in most cases.

To solve this problem a tenant is entitled to an injunction (*see* Chapter 2, People on Your Property for similar examples). This law also now applies to those who have a mere licence as opposed to a tenancy or lease. The tenant's entitlement to an injunction, may be

- because of trespass on his property (since the landlord has no right to be there under a proper lease – he has granted the tenant exclusive possession)
- because the landlord may have created a situation which would constitute nuisance (*see* Chapter 3, Trouble with Your Neighbours)
- because the landlord may well be in breach of contract, since all leases contain a clause saying that the landlord will guarantee quiet enjoyment of the premises, whether such a clause is written into the lease or not
- because the landlord fails to obtain a court order but still evicts the tenant. An injunction can be obtained to make the landlord allow the tenant back into the property, since most tenants can only be evicted by a court order.

RECOVERING POSSESSION OF THE PROPERTY

It is standard practice to take a deposit from the tenant before he moves in from which you can recover compensation for any damage done to your property during the tenancy, and any further compensation can be recovered with a simple county court action (*see* Chapter 7, Resolving Disputes).

There can be complications when you wish to evict a tenant, either during the currency of the lease, or after the lease has expired. Much depends on what kind of lease your tenant has, especially regarding any security of tenure that he gains from that lease. It is more than a matter of the tenant having breached one of the clauses of the lease, the lease expiring or the lease being brought to an end by your serving a notice requiring possession of the property or notice to quit in the case of a tenancy.

Licences

There might be a contract between the landlord and the licensee for the use of the property; this is between the landlord and the licensee who originally agreed the contract, and so cannot attach to others who might come to be landlord and tenant later.

The normal rules of contract apply, and the licensee can recover damages against the landlord for any losses he sustains. Despite this, he would generally have difficulty persuading a court to order the landlord to let him carry on living in the landlord's property.

Termination of a licence

- The licensee should be given a reasonable amount of time to leave the premises, taking into account the moving of their belongings and whether they have a new place to go to.
- You should use the form of notice terminating a licence in case of later court proceedings to satisfy the judge that you were fair in ending the licence.

If the licensee refuses to leave within a reasonable amount of time after the notice has been served on him, you will need a court order to evict him.

Exceptions to this requirement of a court order:
- where the licensee lives with the landlord
- where the licensee lives with a member of the landlord's family and the landlord lives in the same building
- where the licence was only granted for the purposes of a rent-free holiday.

This does not give you the right to use reasonable force to evict the licensee as a trespasser (*see* Chapter 2, People on Your Property).

Termination of tenancies and leases

Tenancies are ended in much the same way as licences.

The landlord must serve a notice to quit and obtain a court order if the tenant still refuses to leave. Force still cannot be used. Thus the only significant difference between tenancies and licences is that during a tenancy the landlord and tenant may change but the tenancy will continue to exist.

When the tenant has a lease, with a fixed date on which it will end, the landlord must serve a notice on the tenant informing them that the landlord requires possession of the property. This must be served at least one rental period in advance of the date that the landlord requires the return of his house or flat (subject to minimum periods). The tenant may need at least three months' notice if the rent is payable quarterly.

The notice may also need to take a particular form, depending on the kind of lease that exists.

Under an assured shorthold tenancy (or short assured tenancy in Scotland) the notice must be served at least two months before possession is required, so that it may need to be served while the lease is still running. The notice can be in a similar form to a notice requiring possession.

Assured tenancies require two weeks' notice, unless Grounds 1, 2, 6, 9 or 16 are to be relied upon (see Other grounds for possession, page 99), in which case the period is also two months. Rent Act tenants must be given a minimum of four weeks' notice. The notice terminating the lease under Rent Act or assured tenancies must be in a form prescribed by law, available from a legal stationer, since these are tenancies which normally give rise to security of tenure.

The landlord will normally require a court order for possession where the tenant remains in the property after the lease has ended, less likely in the case of assured shorthold tenancies. When a lease is in force there are a number of grounds for possession by the landlord which generally depend on the type of lease that was granted in the first place. The most common ground, which applies to all leases, is that the tenant has not kept up with the rent payments. It is often up to the court to decide whether it would be reasonable for the landlord to regain possession.

The lease may give the tenant further security of tenure after it has ended so the landlord will still require grounds for possession. This will not normally be the case with an assured shorthold tenancy, unless the procedure regarding the notice (*see* Assured shorthold tenancies, page 85) was not complied with properly, thus creating an assured tenancy. Once the lease has expired all that is required for repossession is another form of notice to be served on the tenant in advance of when the landlord requires the property. However, as with most leases, unless the tenant wishes to leave voluntarily, a court order is required for the landlord to regain possession.

When the tenant may end the lease The tenant may wish to leave the property before the expiry of the lease. Most leases contain a 'break clause' in the tenant's favour so that he can terminate the lease upon giving notice in a specified amount of time before he wishes to leave.

If the lease contains no such clause then the tenant may still be able to sublet or 'sell' the lease on to someone else, providing this is not in breach of the terms of the lease. Failing these, the tenant may 'surrender' the lease by an agreement in writing with the landlord.

When the landlord may end the lease A lease may contain a 'break' clause stating that the landlord may terminate the lease before it has expired, upon giving a certain period of notice (minimum four weeks) to the tenant. This can only be enforced against the tenant if one of the grounds for possession applies (*see* Other Grounds for Possession, page 99).

- A landlord is not entitled to terminate an assured shorthold tenancy within the first six months of is running. No grounds are needed for assured shorthold tenancies once the lease has come to the end of its fixed term.
- A landlord will be seeking to recover possession of the property once the lease has expired. Unless the lease was an assured shorthold tenancy, he will need to show one of the grounds of possession (*see* pages 100-101), since the tenant gains 'security of tenure' at the end of the lease.

Non-payment of rent
This is the most common ground for possession, although proceedings for possession should not be started as soon as the tenant goes into arrears.

The court is unlikely to even consider granting the landlord possession until there are arrears of at least eight weeks. They might make an order but suspend its operation to give the tenant the chance to pay off the arrears in (usually small) instalments.

Given the substantial amount of time that it can take for the matter to come before the court, landlords should always try to negotiate an arrangement with the tenant for the payment of the arrears themselves.

Many landlords depend on rent for their income though, and perhaps to pay the mortgage on their property. Where the lease is an assured tenancy the landlord has a right to possession when the bank or building society that gave the mortgage seeks possession of the property from the landlord. Once possession has been obtained, the landlord can still seek to recover the rent arrears in a county court debt action (*see* Chapter 7, Resolving Disputes).

Non-payment of bills

A lease would normally provide for the tenant to pay the bills for gas and electricity, although this can be included as a 'blank charge' in the rent. Often it is the landlord who actually pays the bills, but he then recovers the cost from the tenant.

Where the tenant fails to pay the bill, and refuses to pay when he is asked, the landlord must not cut off the gas or electricity, since the tenant will have a right to utilities such as gas and electricity. The courts may see this as a breach of the tenant's right to quiet enjoyment of the property, or even an attempted unlawful eviction. The best solution would be to sue the tenant for the amount of the bill.

Other grounds for possession

These depend on the kind of lease that the tenant has over the property. In an assured shorthold tenancy no grounds for possession are needed once the fixed term has come to an end, since the tenant gains no security of tenure. Therefore the court must grant possession if the lease comes under this head, although you will still normally need a court order. In the other forms of leases the landlord will need to rely on certain grounds. These grounds are listed below by the number by which the courts will know them.

Where the landlord requires possession of the property while the lease is running, then the tenant has to be in breach of one or more of the clauses of the lease, if the clause involves one of the grounds for possession listed below.

To gain possession where the lease is an assured tenancy, the landlord must always show that there is a ground for possession. Many of the first set of grounds require the landlord to give notice to the tenant of the situation before the granting of the lease. If the first set of grounds can be proved and the landlord has followed the correct procedure before granting the lease, then the court must grant possession.

Ground 1   The house was previously the landlord's main residence, and he now needs it for himself or for his wife.

Ground 2   The bank or building society that provided the mortgage for the property requires possession of that property.

Ground 3   The property is normally let for holiday purposes, but the tenant acquired an assured tenancy in it outside the holiday season.

Ground 6   The landlord needs to demolish or reconstruct the property and cannot do this with the tenant residing in the property. (This ground if effective without being communicated to the tenant by written notice before the lease is granted.)

Ground 8   There are substantial rent arrears: at least 13 weeks if the rent is payable weekly and three months if it is payable monthly.

The following are grounds where the court may grant the landlord repossession of the property if it considers it reasonable to do so:

Rent act

If the tenancy was created before 15 January 1989 and is therefore most likely to have been granted under the Rent Act 1977, there are similar grounds for possession, which must also be relied on. The grounds are called 'Cases' under the Rent Act and are also divided into those grounds where the court must grant the landlord possession, and those where the court may grant possession if it thinks that it is reasonable.

Ground 9   Where the landlord can show that the tenant has suitable alternative accommodation to go to if the possession order is granted.

Ground 10   There are some rent arrears (not as serious as Ground 8).

Ground 11   The tenant is persistently late in paying rent.

Ground 12   Breach of the terms of the lease.

Ground 13   The tenant has allowed the house to deteriorate beyond the expected fair wear and tear.

Ground 14   The tenant has annoyed the neighbours so that they might have grounds for action (*see* Chapter 3, Trouble with Your Neighbours).

Ground 15   The tenant has damaged the furniture let with the house.

Ground 16   The tenant was a former employee of the landlord, but that employment has now ended.

The following are where the judge has a discretion as to whether the landlord should regain his property where it is let under a Rent Act lease:

Case 1   The tenant has failed to pay his rent or he is in breach of another clause in the lease.

Case 2 The tenant has annoyed the neighbours to the extent that they might have grounds for action or the tenant has used the property for immoral purposes. (*See* Chapter 3, Trouble with Your Neighbours.)

Case 3 The tenant has allowed the house to deteriorate beyond what might be expected.

Case 4 The tenant has allowed the furniture to deteriorate beyond what might be expected.

Case 5 The tenant has given the landlord a notice to quit the lease, and the landlord faces difficulty if he does not have possession (such as where he has agreed to sell the property).

Case 6 The tenant has sublet the property without the consent of the landlord.

Case 8 The house is needed for an employee of the landlord.

Case 9 The house is needed for the landlord himself.

Case 10 The tenant is overcharging subtenants in the property (where he was allowed to sublet).

The grounds where the court must grant repossession are:

Case 11 The property was formerly the landlord's home and he now requires it for himself or a member of his family. Notice of this should normally have been served on the tenant when he was granted the lease.

Case 13 The property is normally let for holiday purposes, but the tenant acquired an assured tenancy in it outside the holiday season.

The procedure to gain possession

Before any proceedings can start in respect of a lease, the landlord must serve notice to the tenant that he requires vacant possession of the property. The notices for the various kinds of tenancies can be obtained from legal stationers.

Assured shorthold tenancies

• The notice must be served at least two months before possession is required.

Remember that the landlord cannot gain possession in the first six months of the tenancy, but he can serve notice before four months has passed if he wishes to gain repossession immediately after this six-month period.

• If no notice is served during the fixed term, the tenant is entitled to remain in the property after the lease has come to an end.
• If the notice is served after the fixed term has ended, the situation becomes similar to a periodic tenancy, granted week by week or month by month depending on when the rent is due. Thus the tenancy can only end on a rent day at least two months after a notice is served out of the fixed term.

Assured tenancies

The same rules apply as for assured shorthold tenancies except that only two weeks' notice is needed when the landlord is relying on the holiday accommodation rule, any rent arrears, or the 'bad tenant' rules in 3, 4, and 5 of the discretionary rules above.

Rent Act tenancies

These normally require four weeks' notice although again its effect will depend on how frequently the rent is paid.

If the tenant has still failed to move out after the notice period has expired then the landlord can start the court proceedings. (*See* Chapter 7, Resolving Disputes.)

How to resist possession proceedings

Tenants who are the subject of court proceedings or threatened court proceedings under a notice should consider their position carefully. The rules that have been outlined in this chapter are strictly applied by the court and the landlord should have complied with them precisely, depending on which kind of lease is operating.

Consider also whether these rules which give the landlord favourable terms (such as the notice procedure creating an assured shorthold tenancy) are strictly applied; if there is any defect, then you may be in a stronger position.

Note If it appears that you are likely to be evicted if the landlord goes ahead with court proceedings, remember that the landlord can get the court to order that you must pay the costs of bringing the action against you if he is successful. The court is normally the only resort that the landlord has and so any threats to take you to court are to be taken seriously.

Squatters

If squatters have moved into a property that you own, the legal solutions are rather different, since there is no proper landlord-and-tenant relationship. The squatters are effectively mere trespassers. But you will again need a court order to evict them from your property; you cannot treat them as ordinary trespassers and use reasonable force to eject them from the property. Special procedures apply to them. (See Dealing with squatters, page 34, and Chapter 7, Resolving Disputes.)

CHAPTER 6

Making Changes to Your Home

Making changes to your home can be a complex procedure in itself, and you must consider the effect that any change might have on your neighbours, and whether your local planning authority will allow it.

We are dealing here mainly with those who own their property outright, or on freehold, because tenants are normally restricted by a clause in their lease from making alterations to their property unless they obtain the landlord's written consent. There is less incentive to do so under a lease, since the entire property will return to the ownership of the landlord when the lease expires or the landlord repossesses the property. If you have a long lease you may decide that it is worthwhile, but check the provisions of your lease before undertaking any work.

There are elements of both private and public law here.

- Your neighbour might have a specific right to light.
- There may be a special covenant attached to the rights to your property and your neighbour's property restricting what the neighbours can do.
- There may be conditions on the appearance of your property if you have a lease rather than a freehold.
- There are planning and building regulations which govern what may be done to your home and how these changes are effected. Planning laws take into account what the neighbours might say about your

changes; they will often be specific to your area so that any changes do not affect the character of your neighbourhood.

PRIVATE RIGHTS CONTROLLING CHANGES TO YOUR HOME

Particular rights attached to your property

Apart from under the general planning laws, you can only put a stop to the construction of a new property or extension near you if it affects a particular right that you have. The same applies when you wish to build an extension but your neighbour objects.

General rights

In law you have no general right to light nor to privacy. Sometimes you might be able to assert a right to light, where this might be seen as a special feature of the property and if this right has existed in respect of your property for as long as can be remembered.

You would need to show that the right to light has existed for at least 20 years; therefore there was nothing that might have stopped you or the then owners of that property from enjoying the right to light for that length of time.

Beware The procedure for proving a successful claim of this sort is both limited and complicated. If you believe that it would still be worth your while then you should consult a solicitor regarding any assertion of your right to light.

Possibly a right to light is expressly incorporated into the deeds of the property. There may be provisions and your neighbour
- may not be able to build on a certain area of his property
- may not be able to raise an existing building any higher
- may not do anything else which might interfere with the light coming to your house.

Again, there is also no general legal recognition of a right to privacy. If planning permission is required, the planning authority will consider any effect that a new building or extension will have on the surrounding area, including privacy and the light coming to neighbouring properties.

Previous agreements – England and Wales

Restrictive covenants A more specific right can arise if there has been an agreement between the owners of properties as to what might be built in the future and what will not. The agreements attach to the property itself and so are normally still enforceable when the ownership of either property has changed hands. However, these 'restrictive covenants' can sometimes be set aside by the courts or the Lands Tribunal if the character of the neighbourhood has changed since the agreement was reached or if they have not been enforced at all in the past.

Examples

- There might be a covenant against 'alterations', prohibiting new windows, doors and walls, thus possibly precluding the property being converted into flats.
- It might be that the property may only be used for residential purposes, and not business, so that even taking in holiday guests or letting out part of the house as a flat is not allowed.
- There could be a covenant which requires all conversion or improvement plans to be submitted to and approved by the owner of the neighbouring property and his approval obtained before going ahead with the alterations.

A standard clause in most leases is that the tenant will not make any alterations or additions to the property that has been leased. This can be useful to a landlord who lets out part of his property but chooses to live in the other part, i.e. next to the tenant.

Other examples of this relate to how the tenant chooses to keep the appearance of the property. Clauses may strictly set out what the tenant can and can't do in terms of decoration (internal or external) so that the general appearance of the neighbourhood is not adversely affected.

Restrictive covenants are powerful when they work, and will even overrule the district council's grant of planning permission in respect of intended building works. But it is up to the person who now owns the land which has the benefit of the covenant to enforce that covenant. In the event that the owners of the other property will not cooperate an injunction from the court is available to stop the construction or conversion of the building taking place.

Real burdens and conditions – Scotland

The Scottish equivalents of restrictive covenants are the burdens and conditions contained in the title deeds to the property. These are rights and obligations imposed on the buyer of any property in Scotland at the time of purchase. They can only be enforced by the person who sold you the property, although sometimes, where it is specifically included in the deeds, neighbours may also have the right to enforce them. Matters addressed could be what developments can be made to the property, and the insurance and maintenance of the property. The burdens and conditions on any property in Scotland can be found in the 'Burdens section' in the title deeds.

Breach of the conditions can mean that those affected might obtain an injunction or damages – for example, where a condition requires contribution to the upkeep of a communal area, and the owner fails to pay. In some circumstances, where it is specifically provided in what is known as an 'irritant and resolutive clause', the property can be repossessed by those who retain the right under the Scottish system of land law. These are the 'superior' (who originally sold the property at the higher level of the tree) and the 'disponer' (who sold the property to the present owner).

The current owner of a property who is subject to harsh burdens and conditions also has the right to appeal to the Lands Tribunal of Scotland. It is possible that they may be able to get some of the conditions varied if they appear to be out of date or too harsh for the owner to be able to keep to.

London rules

Special rules regarding the alteration and construction of new party walls apply to certain Inner London boroughs, so that legal notices have to be served on the neighbours that are affected. The relevant London boroughs are the City of London, Camden, Greenwich, Hackney, Hammersmith & Fulham, Islington, Kensington & Chelsea, Lambeth, Lewisham, Southwark, Tower Hamlets, Wandsworth and Westminster.

Party walls

If the work that you are to undertake affects a party wall between two properties, you must consider the effects that the work may have on your neighbour's buildings.

- If you deliberately pull down a wall, and this affects your neighbour's right of support such that the structure of his building is damaged, you will be liable to compensate him.
- Demolishing the whole wall, where ownership of it is shared between you, will amount to a trespass, since you will have destroyed part of his property on his land (*see* Walls, page 19).

If you are altering a party wall between properties in any of these London boroughs, then, in the absence of agreement with the owner of the other half of the wall, you must serve a notice on him at least one month before you start the work, specifying exactly what it is that you wish to do. You can obtain the form from the Royal Institute of British Architects (*see* Useful Addresses).

Should you wish to build a wall on the boundary of a property in the London boroughs mentioned, you must always serve a notice. If you wish to build the wall actually on the boundary, so that some of it will be on your neighbour's land, then your neighbour may reply to the notice and give his consent; thus the new wall will become a party wall, so that you both own it.

If he fails to give his consent then you are not entitled to go over the boundary of your land and on to his.

PUBLIC CONTROL OF CHANGES TO YOUR HOME

Planning permission regulations do not just mean that only your local council has the power to decide whether an extension or alteration should go ahead or not; other people such as neighbours will be entitled to object to them and this will be a consideration in the council's decision-making process. The planning authority will let others know of the proposals either by placing a notice on the property concerned, or sometimes by informing and consulting neighbours directly.

You can also inform the planning authority of any breaches of the planning permission once your neighbour has begun work.

Whether planning permission is required

Many alterations, improvements and even extensions can be done without planning permission provided they come within a certain class of development known as the 'permitted development' and conform to certain scales.

Whether permission is required or not depends mainly on the size of the proposed project and the area that you live in. District councils and London boroughs are the institutions that decide whether to give planning permission, and each is entitled to form its own policies and methods of reaching decisions, so long as they are not unreasonable. There is a constant stream of advice and recommendations deriving from central government and may affect the way the planning authority views the application.

Any material change in the use of buildings requires the local authority's permission, such as converting your house from a single dwelling into one designed for more than one family to live in, or if you consider running a hostel, hotel or holiday letting in the property. Sometimes there does not even have to be any alteration to the physical structure of the house.

If you live in a listed building or in an area classified as a conservation area, then it is more likely that you will need planning permission for alterations to your home since many of the permitted developments do not apply in these cases. Check with your planning authority before you make any changes.

If in doubt

If you are in doubt after reading this chapter as to whether you will need planning permission, then you can go and talk to the planning authority anyway to check, as most give general advice during the day. You can ask them for a 'certificate of lawfulness of proposed use or development' as security that no permission is needed, provided you stick to the plans.

Improvements, alterations and extensions

This covers most alterations that involve building work whether it will mean a change in the appearance of the property or not. Planning permission usually will be required for this unless it comes within the definition of 'permitted development'. This depends on the nature of the work, where it is on the property, and how substantial the work is likely to be. For example, erecting a marquee in your garden for a limited amount of time will not require planning permission.

Changes to the interior of your property Any work which will affect only the interior of the building, or at least not materially affect the exterior appearance of the building, is permitted and no planning permission is required. Minor alterations to the outside of the house can be made without planning permission, such as

- repainting the house (as long as you are not creating an advertisement)
- repairing the roof
- repointing the brickwork.

The law looks at the basic theme of the house to decide if the exterior has been materially affected.

This is not carte blanche to go ahead with any plans you had for the inside of the house, since you may be interfering with the structure of the house. Knocking an interior wall down could materially affect the safety of the structure of the building, and so notice should be given to the building

---

Going through the roof

Loft conversions qualify as changes to the interior of your house even if you are adding dormer windows, but you must not change the walls of the property, only the slope of the roof for the purposes of the windows. Remember that you should not make material changes to the exterior of the house without considering whether you need planning permission.

---

inspector at the council before doing this. Building regulations generally apply to all structural changes. (See Building Regulations, page 118). However, you will not actually need planning permission to make such an alteration if it is inside the property.

Any work which may affect party walls which you share with neighbours in terraced or semi-detached houses or flats needs some forethought. The issue of party walls can be sensitive between neighbours and so it may be wise to have someone from the building inspector's office check that you will not do any damage. You may obtain a 'party wall award' where a surveyor from the department inspects your neighbour's property both before and after the work is carried out. He can be testament to the fact that no damage has been caused by the work.

Changes to the exterior of your property You can do less to the outside of your property without the need for planning permission, but your proposals may still come within the 'permitted development' as defined in the General Development Order 1988. If you are planning extensive works, some of which will require permission and some not, then you must still apply for the planning permission before carrying out any of the works. This is because any permission that is granted may yet exclude some of the permitted developments that would normally be allowed under the General Development Order.

Breach of the permission or permitted development
This may be very expensive, as the planning authority has the power to declare that the whole of the works that were carried out are in breach and

not just the part that exceeds the permission or permitted development. Ultimately, the council can require that the whole of the extension or alteration be removed, although they may be willing to forgive if there are no objections.

Extensions

Extensions come within the permitted development provided they are built to a scale proportionate to the house.

- The extension must be no more than a 15 per cent increase on the original building, or an extra 70 cubic metres/2,471 cubic feet (taking an external measurement), whichever is the greater.
- In terraced houses you are allowed 10 per cent or 50 cubic metres/1,765 cubic feet.
- If you are using the percentage measure then there is an absolute maximum of an extra 115 cubic metres/4,061 cubic feet.

The 'original building' for these purposes is not your house as it was just before you built the extension, but the house as it was on 1 July 1948, or as it was originally built if it was constructed after that date.

- The extension must be no higher than the main building, and must be no nearer the road than the main building unless this is still 20 metres/65 feet away.
- If any part of the extension is within 2 metres/6.5 feet of the next-door property then the extension cannot be more than 4 metres/13 feet high.
- the extension is not to take up more than half of the garden as it existed before the extension was built.

If you are planning to build an extension beyond these limits then you will need planning permission. You cannot build two small extensions, one after another, in order to come within the permitted development as the dimensions of the first one would count towards the second. Thus you cannot extend the extension if the whole extension then goes beyond the limits of the permitted development.

Other buildings and structures

Garages are treated as extensions for the purposes of permitted development provided it is attached to the house or no more than 5 metres/16 feet away from the main house. If it is further away than this, it must accord with the regulations that apply to all other so called 'outhouses' such as:

• greenhouses
• garden sheds
• summerhouses
• anything that you might keep animals in such as kennels, rabbit hutches, bee hives and dovecotes.

Outhouses cover other things that might be an extension to the house but are not for living in (as a garage is not for living in), but which are not actually attached to the main building.

The conditions which would keep these structures within the permitted development are as follows:

• It may not be higher than 3 metres/10 feet, or 4 metres/13 feet if the roof is ridged.
• It may not be larger than 10 cubic metres/33 cubic feet if placed within 5 metres/16 feet of the house.
• It must not be nearer the road than the house, or at least 20 metres/65 feet away, nor may it take up more than half of the garden.

Tree houses and **tents** do not require planning permission.

Roof extensions may count as extensions, but are subject to further restrictions before planning permission is required.

• The development is not allowed to go beyond the top or the edges of the existing roof
• The volume space cannot be extended by more than 50 cubic metres/1,765 cubic feet (40 cubic metres/1,412 cubic feet in the case of terraced houses)

Discreet dishes

A satellite dish may be installed on the roof provided it does not go any higher than the highest part of the roof. If you put it on the chimney then the dish is only allowed to be 45 centimetres/18 inches in any direction, but anywhere else the dish can be larger – up to 90 centimetres/35 inches in any direction.

- You can replace the roof as long as the new one is not too different from the previous one
- You can add skylights without planning permission.

Porches can be added without planning permission provided:
- that the floor area is no greater than 3 square metres/32 square feet
- that it is no higher than 3 metres/10 feet above the ground
- that it is not within 2 metres/6.5 feet of the road.

Fences and walls can be a maximum of 2 metres/6.5 feet in height, and only 1 metre/39 inches where it is by a road that is used by vehicles. Exceeding these levels will mean that planning permission is required.

Conversion of the use of the property

If there is a material change of use of your property, the law looks at the extent to which the property has changed, for example allowing someone to park his caravan on your property for a fee would not go over the threshold, whereas developing a caravan site would. You may repair a friend's car in your garage but not set up an entire mechanic's business.

If your house is let as lodgings or a hostel, this is a substantial change in the 'character' of the use of the property. However, infrequently letting it as a holiday home will not amount to a material change of use for which planning permission would be required.

Converting your home into other forms of business, is generally prohibited without planning permission; you are entitled to work from home though, if you only use a living room or spare bedroom as an office.

Conversion of your property into flats may also attract the need for planning permission, although you can convert it for multiple occupation in the same living area provided no more than six people will be living there. The planning authority will assess the suitability of the building for conversion whether:

- it is big enough
- there is a shortage of accommodation in the area
- the neighbourhood can provide for or cope with an increased number of people living in it (for instance, whether there is enough parking in the area).

Obtaining planning permission

Step 1 The planning authority at your local district council or London borough offices will have a standard form of application for planning permission which you must complete and return with a plan of the intended changes.

You will also be required to lodge an ownership certificate to say that you are indeed the owner, a copy of which can be obtained from the planning department or legal stationers. You will be asked to pay a fee, which will vary according to the kind of work done. The fees that are relevant for the purposes of this book are as follows (with effect from January 1995):

Extensions, improvements and other alterations to a single house:	£70.00
Converting a house into separate flats or houses (per new flat):	£140.00
Changing the use of the house from residential to business:	£140.00

Step 2 The planning authority will then publicise the application, either by a notice on the property concerned, or by notifying the neighbours by letter. It is at this stage that anyone who wishes to object should let the district council know of their concerns.

Step 3 The planning authority will make its decision in accordance with the council's adopted development plan, and should let you know what decision it has reached within eight weeks of receiving the complete application (form, certificate of ownership, and fee).

Appeal Only the applicant has the right to appeal (where the permission is refused); an objector has no right to appeal against the decision to grant permission. To appeal, the applicant must deliver a notice of appeal to the Department of the Environment in a standard form.

Step 4 When permission is granted the planning authority may impose conditions or may grant it unconditionally.

Go ahead with your plans, but be aware of the time limit on the permission (normally five years, but any conditions may specify otherwise). Your only other concerns are the building regulations.

Objecting to planning permission

The purpose of the planning authority's notices or informing of occupants of nearby houses is to sound out the concerns of the neighbours. However, the council is concerned primarily with effecting its 'development plan' and will apply the policies it has adopted in the past. The personal circumstances of a neighbour (such as any threat to the value of his house were permission granted) are not paramount, though they can certainly swing a decision. When the concerns surround the threat to privacy (relating to the building of an extension) or quiet enjoyment of the area (relating to an application for change of use of a property), then greater weight will be given to any objections that are received.

Any objections that are received (best in writing) at the planning authority offices within 21 days after the notices are put up or received, must be considered before any decision is made as to whether planning permission is granted.

Objectors are normally notified of the outcome of the decision by the planning authority, although this is a matter of practice rather than law.

The objector has no right to appeal a grant of planning permission unless it is plainly unreasonable. Where they consider that no reasonable planning authority could have come to such a decision, or that the authority granted permission from some ulterior motive (outside its own planning policy) then they have the right to seek judicial review of the decision. The procedure for doing this is outside the scope of this book.

Objecting to other developments in the area

Another area where there may be objection is the granting of licences to pubs, restaurants, clubs and sex shops; these licences are granted by magistrates at a special hearing in the court.

Notice of the hearing has to be put on the door of the premises 28 days before the date of the licensing sessions, and advertised in the local newspapers. You may then attend the hearing to give evidence as to why the licence should not be granted; you do not need to give any prior warning that you will object when the licence is being made for the first time.

Renewal of an existing licence

Here you must put your objections in writing and give them to the clerk at the magistrate's court and the applicant no later than a week before the hearing.

You should then also attend at the hearing of the renewal, which will normally be at the general annual licensing meeting. These are held each year at the court and will be announced in local newspapers. The time, date and place that the meeting will be held will all be stated so that you can attend in order to put forward any objections you may have. Magistrates have the power to impose conditions on the licence, such as the number of opening hours.

Building regulations

Any construction of a building or extension, or alteration to the structure of an existing building or extension (internal or external), must conform to the building regulations. It also requires authorisation by the building department of your local district or borough council.

Exceptions
- putting in double glazing
- putting in central heating
- insulating the property
- installing a replacement in exactly the same place (such as a new sink).

Bear in mind that you will still need to follow the regulations even though you do not need the council's consent.

Also consider the fact that these are not absolute exceptions: you may well wish to make alterations to the structure of your house in the process of installation of any of the above, in which case you will also need consent.

The regulations exist to ensure that there are good standards of building work throughout the country relating to structure, fire safety, insulation, ventilation, hygiene, drainage, and facilities for the disabled. They are similar to enforced codes of practice but they apply to anyone who undertakes the building work.

The regulations require:
- That the work is carried out in accordance with the specifications.
- That the plans for the proposed building work are approved by the inspectors. The inspectors can be either part of your local district council or can be private inspectors approved by the Department of the Environment, designated bodies such as the Royal Institution of Chartered Surveyors, or corporate bodies such as the National House-Building Council. You will have to negotiate a fee with the private inspectors for approval of your plans, whereas the district council has set fees depending on the value of the work that is to be carried out.

A builder doing your works will normally sort out the regulations as part of his contract. His failure to conform with the regulations will still have major implications for you.

If you plan to undertake the work yourself, then the regulations still have to be complied with. You must deposit the plans with the district council building department or an approved inspector (or with any

> ### Put to the test
>
> The only building works to which the building regulations do not apply are
> structures such as greenhouses, porches, covered yards and detached buildings
> with no sleeping quarters where the floor space does not cover more than 30
> square metres/323 square feet. Most work you carry out on your home where
> the structure is affected will probably be subject to the regulations.

application for planning permission to the planning department) before
you commence the work. If the building inspector does not reject the
plans within ten days then you are entitled to presume that they are
accepted. Otherwise they may make changes to your plans and set out
ways in which you can conform to the regulations.

To know whether your plans come within the regulations, the best book
to look at is the *Manual to the Building Regulations* published by HMSO.
It gives a good commentary in layman's terms if you plan to carry out the
work yourself.

Enforcement of the building regulations Naturally, the works that are
carried out must then conform to those plans and the regulations. Once
the work has been completed the inspector will grant a final or completion
certificate. Any breach of the rules may be enforced in one of three ways.

1 The local authority may serve a 'section 36 notice' on the building
   which requires that the illegal work is removed, or that the work is
   altered to comply with the rules. You will be given 28 days to do
   either of these, after which the local authority has the power to
   remove the offending work and charge you for the cost of doing so. If
   you need more time then you can make an application to the
   magistrates' court for an extension.

   Alternatively, when you receive a section 36 notice you can obtain
   (upon payment of a fee) a report from a qualified building engineer to
   say that the work is adequate in the form that it originally took. The
   local authority may then be persuaded to withdraw the notice and
   may even refund the cost of the expert.

2 The magistrates can also seek to take criminal proceedings against you in the magistrates' court if you fail to conform to the regulations. The court can impose a fine of £50 for every day that the work continues to offend the rules.

3 Anyone (including the local authority) can get an injunction against you; this is unlikely.

CHAPTER 7

Resolving Disputes

Disputes between neighbours can be famously protracted, often leading to serious acrimony between the parties, and continuing for many months, sometimes years. Often these result from a pride in one's own home, and a desire to preserve ideals of peace and quiet enjoyment of your property. In many cases the best thing is to grin and bear it. It is vital that people consider the matter as objectively as possible and try to come to some agreement about whatever causes a grievance.

The law seeks to preserve a balance between people's interests on all occasions. The court will frequently refrain from giving a clear-cut decision, but instead urge compromise between the parties and impose conditions on both of them. Going to court should be your very last resort. If you fail to agree among yourselves there are other means of settling a dispute.

WAYS OF SETTLING DISPUTES WITHOUT LITIGATION

Your local council

The council have obligations towards 'the public health' and 'the promotion or protection of the interests of the inhabitants' of their area. They may also try to offer means of ending the dispute, since they can see the problem objectively.

Reaching agreement through mediation

It may be possible to settle disputes formally without litigation. Agreements can often be reached through mediators, which will always be cheaper than solicitors. It is sensible to put any agreements reached into writing so that you both know where you are if something arises in the future. A common example of this is an agreement regarding the ownership and responsibility for a party wall between two properties.

Legal aid

Find out whether you are entitled to legal aid before using the court system, unless you are happy to go ahead with the application yourself without using lawyers. Entitlement to civil legal aid has been substantially reduced over the years, but many people remain eligible. Legal aid may be granted for a solicitor to handle certain applications, although the litigant may be required to make a contribution to the legal costs that are incurred.

The Legal Aid Board can recover any costs it has paid for on your behalf out of any money that you recover, unless you can get the judge to order that your legal costs be paid for by the other party. This will normally happen if you win the case outright, and if there is little evidence that the other party tried to settle the dispute with reasonable offers to you before going to court. However, if you are claiming under £1,000 or using the arbitration option then no costs can be awarded to the winning party. It will not normally be worth looking for legal aid here.

There are two types of legal aid: the Green Form Scheme and full civil legal aid.

The Green Form Scheme This allows general advice and the drafting of documents up to a maximum of two hours of the solicitor's time. This can be useful for drafting the particulars of claims that are required in most possession actions and all injunction applications. It will normally be up to you to represent yourself at the hearing after that.

You will automatically qualify for the Green Form Scheme advice and assistance if you are in receipt of income support, family credit or disability working allowance, provided you have no more than £1,000 in capital not including the value of your home and its contents (£1,335 if you have one dependant, and £1,535 if you have two dependants).

Failing that, you are ineligible if you earn more than £70 per week, although again you are given more scope if you have dependants. An allowance of £26 per week is made for a partner, and anything from £15 to £36 per week for dependants depending on their age.

Full civil legal aid gives you not only the preliminary legal advice and assistance before the court hearing, but also representation in court by a solicitor or barrister.

All those in receipt of income support are eligible for civil legal aid, regardless of capital (although this may change soon). For those not on income support the limits are as follows:

Income: £7,060 per year, but pay a contribution after £2,382 per year
Capital: £6,750, but pay a contribution after £3,000.

Again you are allowed certain amounts to be disregarded if you have dependants to look after, and there are allowances for pensioners with high capital. If your claim is for personal injury then the limits are slightly increased:

Income: £7,780 per year, with the same contribution limit
Capital: £8,560, with the same contribution limit.

If you think that you are entitled to legal aid and the claim is complicated or valuable, then see a solicitor or a Citizens' Advice Bureau who will help to complete the forms for you to apply to the Legal Aid Board.

GOING TO COURT

Principles of the court system and other considerations
England and Wales The county court system in was set up for litigants-in-person. The court staff are generally helpful to those who are not versed in the procedure and other formalities and the judges are specially trained now to deal with litigants-in-person. They will always be sympathetic to

those who are not legally represented, giving them every opportunity to put their case and letting them know what they have to do. The court system has introduced a system of arbitration, where legal fees cannot be recovered from the party who loses, in order to try to discourage the use of solicitors and barristers.

Scotland The sheriff's court is the equivalent for this kind of matter. Additionally, you need to state on the initial writ the bases of law under which you seek the assistance of the court. Since the court cannot decide the matter unless these are in order, it may be best to get some advice regarding these 'pleas-in-law'. A Citizens' Advice Bureau or the court staff may help you. Again, the system is straightforward and sympathetic to those seeking justice without the use of lawyers.

Going to court can be confusing, time-consuming and expensive. Avoid going to court unless absolutely necessary, and try to come to some agreement with the person or persons you are in dispute with, or, failing that try your local council. However, in some cases a court order will be necessary.

You have a limited time in which to decide whether you should go to court or not. The law weeds out those cases which it views as stale and which should have been brought at an earlier stage. In most of the situations covered in Chapters 2, 3 and 4, an action must be brought within six years from the date when you knew that your neighbour was causing a problem which caused you either inconvenience or annoyance, or damage to any of your property. However, you have only three years in cases where you suffered any kind of personal injury. Injury can cover mental stress leading to substantial medical consequences, although you need to get a doctor to back you up in writing in all cases where any kind of injury is caused.

Most neighbour disputes will be more urgent than this. If you do not act quickly then the threatened damage may already have been done by the time you come to court. In some very urgent situations you are allowed to go before a judge to get an order without even telling the other side that you are doing this. However, after making any order the judge will want to get the parties together as soon as possible to hear what the other side has to say about the problem (normally within a week or two).

The law is very reluctant to decide on a matter at court when it appears that either or both sides do not know exactly what is the case against them. A judge will become very impatient when he or she finds that somebody has been hiding a crucial fact from the other party just so that no decision can properly be made. Before going to court, parties normally have to prepare their case on paper, and must let both the judge and the other side see any documents that may be relevant. That way, the full story will be known and any chance of settling out of court can be given a full run. Any attempts to settle the case before coming to court will be viewed favourably by the judge and give you more credibility, so offers of compromise ought to be in writing.

Consider what you have actually lost

If you have suffered damage or personal injury and the other side refuses to accept the blame or will not voluntarily pay compensation, then the court may be a valid option. Where it is your feelings that have been hurt, or you think that your privacy has been violated, then there is little that the court can do. People often talk about 'their rights', but the court does not think that way – it looks to redress matters of injustice (to either party) that might apply generally to anyone. There are set formulae where wrongful acts have cost you money or caused you physical harm, but there is less that you can do about a mere sense of injustice.

Going to court – preliminary considerations

There are many hurdles that litigation places in front of you. These are partly so that the court can get a proper objective view of the situation, but partly to encourage you to take a different perspective of the problem, and therefore perhaps reach a compromise. If you choose to see a solicitor to help you with the procedure, there is a good chance that he or she may offer an alternative way of resolving the issue.

You must decide which court it is that will help you. Most domestic non-criminal matters are dealt with in the county court, although a magistrates' court also deals with some matters such as noise. There are many county courts throughout England and Wales, but the one that you must use is the one that covers the area in which the person you plan to sue lives.

The person you wish to sue (the defendant) also has to be considered. Of course you can sue more than one person in the same matter, but it is safest just to go for the one you are sure is responsible. If they have to pay any compensation to you, you can let them recover the cost from anyone else who might be liable. However, if you seek an injunction, you must include all those you think ought to be stopped from whatever it is they are doing. If you seek a repossession order against tenants, then all the tenants you wish to sue need to be in your application to the court.

Another hurdle may be finding the name or address of the defendant. In the event of your trying to sue a child (a defendant under the age of 18)

Variable fees

The court will require a fee to be paid, which you can normally recover if you win the case. This fee will depend on the value of the action and the amount that is being claimed if it is for the payment of money:

Actions for money (minimum fee £10):	
up to £600	10p per pound claimed
between £600.01 and £1,000	£65
between £1,000.01 and £5,000	£70
over £5,000	£80
Injunctions and originating applications alone	£50
Injunctions with a claim for money	
under £500	£50
over £500	as with money claims above
Service of documents by court bailiff	£10 per defendant
Setting down your case for trial	£50

the court will need to ensure that a guardian is appointed, to protect the child's interests.

Procedure for going to court

To start the action you will need to go to the county court and pick up an application form for a summons (a document that starts off the court proceedings), or originating application.

An application form for a summons is known as a 'Request for issue of the summons' since it is the court itself which issues the summons. Where the claim is for money alone (as in compensation) you want a 'default summons'; ask for a small claims form if the amount will be less than £1,000. But if you seek anything else, such as an injunction, or both an injunction and compensation, then you should ask for a 'fixed date summons'.

If you are a landlord and you seek either possession of your property or rent arrears from your tenants, these have their own special procedure (*see* Recovery of money, page 131).

A further type of application is an originating application, but this can be used only if you need the court to interpret deeds to a property that is the subject of a dispute, and nothing more than that – it may be the case that everything else will turn on how the court views these documents, and so this will be quicker and cheaper. The county court staff will help, making sure you use the correct method of starting an action, and showing you what to do.

The forms are to request that the county court issues the summons on your behalf, but you must fill in the relevant parts (there are notes for guidance) to state what you claim and why. The court will deal with the matter on your behalf, once you have paid the fee for the issue of the summons, including posting the summons to the defendant.

It is then up to the defendant to either admit the claim, dispute the amount you claim, or dispute their liability towards you altogether. If they admit the claim completely, or fail to do anything within two weeks of the date when they should have received the summons, then you can return to court and request judgement.

Arbitration

Should the defendant dispute your claim, the matter is taken further. If the claim is for less than £1,000 and there is no request for an injunction, then it will automatically go to arbitration (also known as the small claims court). This is a much less formal sort of court hearing, at which you can still represent yourself or be represented by a friend who is not a lawyer. No legal costs can be recovered by either of the parties. It is often wise to request that the matter goes to arbitration so that the use of lawyers is discouraged, and costs are kept to a minimum.

If the matter is to go further, the court will send you instructions, particularly regarding the lodging of relevant documents at court, so that the whole matter can be put before the judge in the case. It also means that the other side has a chance to see what your case is, and vice versa.

The court hearing

On the day of the hearing you should arrive at court in good time and make sure that any witnesses that you have know where and when to go. You will invariably find that there will be many other cases listed in the same slot. This is because the court expects many cases to settle at the door of the court, but it cannot be predicted which ones will do this. You must therefore be prepared for a long wait.

When your case is called in, you may take your witnesses with you. However, if the hearing is in chambers, it will be best to leave them in the waiting area for the moment, so that they can be called when they are needed. The court may sit in either a full court room, or, especially if it is a district judge who will hear the matter, in the judge's chambers. All arbitrations are with a district judge in chambers (which means that you sit round a table). The procedure will be much more informal.

If you are in a court room, the two parties should sit in the front bench, and stand when they are speaking and when the judge comes in or goes out of the court room.

Where there are no lawyers on either side, then the hearing will always be relatively informal.

The judge will have seen the papers relating to the case which you and the other party gave to the court before the trial. He will conduct the hearing himself, asking if you have any witnesses or any proposals for settling the matter at this late stage.

It is the person who brought the action (the plaintiff) who starts with his evidence and then the defendant who replies to it with any witnesses he may have. The judge will decide what is to happen in the course of the hearing if he thinks this is appropriate.

Both of the parties will normally be witnesses themselves, and the judge may ask you questions if you need to give any evidence. Remember that you do technically have to prove everything either by the papers that are brought to court or by the evidence of witnesses. For example, if you suffered an injury which has since disappeared, then you should have your GP as a witness. All witnesses can be cross-examined by the other party after they have given their evidence for the party they support. The judge will probably have further questions after that. At the end the judge will give his decision and the court will draw up any order that is made.

Scottish litigation procedure

Litigation in matters that concern us here should be commenced in the local sheriff's court. You need to complete an initial writ, which can be written out yourself on any A4 sheet of paper, although it must conform to the correct layout (samples are available from any legal stationers).

The facts that gave rise to your action should be outlined as concisely as possible under the 'condescendence'. The pleas-in-law are the bases of law in which you state your claim. To check on these you will probably need to consult a lawyer – perhaps a friend or someone at a legal advice centre if you do not wish to instruct solicitors.

You or your solicitors then sign the warrant and present it to the sheriff's clerk, who will check that it is in order, and then grant a warrant to cite the defender. The defender then has 21 days to reply to the writ. The procedures following this are similar to those in English courts.

PARTICULAR COURT PROCEEDINGS

Recovery of money

Where you have suffered due to the fault of somebody else, be it

- damage to your property
- an injury you have sustained
- substantial interference with your home life

you may be entitled to recover money from the person responsible. This is more appropriate when the damage has already been done, rather than when the damage is threatened by the behaviour and actions of the person who is at fault. There are set guidelines on what sort of behaviour can lead to your basis for compensation and on what sort of thing you can recover compensation for, which often depends on the problem that arose.

For instance, except in the case of trespass and where loss to you was intended, it is very difficult to recover any money unless you have suffered actual damage to your property or injury to yourself. No one else may claim for the damage or injury done to you or recover compensation for any losses they suffered which happened to result from that damage or injury. For example, your employer cannot sue the same person for the lost time while you recovered from your injury. In proving the damage was predictable, (*see* page 63), it must also have been possible to predict that this kind of damage might happen given the set of circumstances that were created. So anything which is damaged that is rather out-of-the-ordinary may well be excluded from the compensation. The law basically wishes to make people pay for the damage which they ought to have been able to foresee in a normal situation.

If you have suffered property damage, then the cost is generally recoverable. But the law's aim is to put you back in the position you were in before the damage was caused. For example, if you lent your neighbour your old lawn-mower and he then broke it, you will not get the cost of a brand new lawn-mower, only the value of the old one. You are entitled to recover the cost of renting a new one in the meantime but you cannot just go out and rent the most expensive one on the market. If one is available to borrow without causing any problems, then you will be unlikely to recover the cost of hiring since that would be seen as unnecessary in the circumstances – this is known as 'mitigation of damage'.

If you have suffered an injury the court may also make a monetary award in your favour. The court looks at your age, and any effects that it had on you or your everyday life and work, and then decides on a lump-sum award. You should therefore not bother about scratches and grazes,

---

Typical awards

The following are a few examples of the sorts of awards that are made for certain injuries, depending on the circumstances of the injured person.

A female state-enrolled nurse, aged 55, suffered bruising and severe swelling on her left thigh and calf when a fire extinguisher fell on her leg because the hospital had not made sure it was properly attached to the wall. Her leg was in bandages for two weeks; she found it difficult to move about for the first week and had to take four and a half weeks off work. For the pain and the injury (not for any lost wages) the court awarded her £950 at today's prices.

A male yard hand, aged 37, endured a ragged laceration to his left index finger, which required five stitches, and left a small permanent scar. He also found it difficult to move his finger for a long period. He was awarded £200.

An elderly lady, aged 89, who had difficulty seeing and hearing, suffered shock when she witnessed her neighbour's Rottweiler dog savage her own dog in her garden on two occasions. Her dog required extensive treatment from the vet. The elderly lady found it difficult to sleep and was reluctant to use her garden ever again because of her distress. She was awarded £200 compensation in 1992.

A 29-year-old male engineer suffered three broken fingers to his left hand, and the nail of his little finger was torn off. He suffered aches and pain during the cold weather as a result of his injury, and there was a risk that he might develop arthritis in the hand. He also had difficulty moving his hand and fingers after that. He was awarded £4,350 at today's prices.

---

unless they are particularly painful. The law follows set guidelines which you can find in most libraries containing legal books.

Recovery of rent arrears is a special kind of court action which the court staff should help you on. You are entitled to all the money that the tenant should have paid you, although he might apply for a 'counterclaim' if he alleges that you as a landlord were also in breach of some of your duties. The court will set off these two claims against each other if it finds that they are both true.

Where someone's actions are causing you substantial inconvenience or are interfering with your quiet enjoyment of your home, then it is rare to seek compensation. It is best dealt with by an injunction while the problem is going on or threatens to continue, rather than by claiming compensation after the problem is over.

On all claims for the recovery of money the court will add interest, currently at 8 per cent per annum, from the date that the damage or injury was caused, or from the dates that the rent was due. This is another incentive for settling the matter out of court, since it can take a long time before you get a hearing date.

Obtaining an injunction

This can be very complicated and expensive, especially since there is no special provision for litigants-in-person. The procedure is not as simple as obtaining an order for the payment of money, and there are many more forms and documents that will have to be completed.

Injunctions should only be used where the problem that is causing you trouble is specific to you. The council will not deem it sufficiently 'public' for them to get involved; nevertheless they are still a good first port-of-call, and may be able to give you advice on how best to deal with it. Finally, there may be a possibility of coming to a compromise.

Applications for injunctions need to be by fixed date summons (*see* page 128), which can also be obtained from the court. You will need also an application for an 'interlocutory injunction', assuming that you wish the problem to be solved immediately. Let the court staff know that you want to make an interlocutory application for an injunction, and get a date for the hearing as soon as possible.

Scotland The application is made on the same form as for money, on Form G1. Applications for an interdict against violence and harassment between spouses or common-law spouses are made on their own special form, and so the situation should be outlined to the court staff.

The application for an interdict will ask you what you want the court to order. Courts have always been reluctant to tell people to do a positive act and only look to order the defendant to refrain from doing something. You should therefore phrase the order in the terms 'the defendant be forbidden from …' as opposed to 'the defendant take such steps as are necessary to …'. Once the papers are completed the court will follow its usual procedure and send the summons and any other documents to the defendant.

If the application is very urgent indeed, then the court may be prepared to make an order without your having to wait to serve the papers on the defendant. This is an *ex parte* order, (or interim interdict in Scotland). It will only take effect for a few days at a time before the matter has to come back before the judge so that he can hear the other side's story.

Note The court is always reluctant to make orders when the other side is not aware that they are even being brought, and so these orders should only be applied for when there is a serious threat to your livelihood where physical injury is in danger of being caused, such as in domestic violence cases.

The reasons for your requiring an injunction will need to be put on a separate document, known as the 'particulars of claim'. These come in a prescribed form and need to include at the end exactly what it is that you are claiming. A solicitor will be helpful here.

The evidence at hearings for injunctions at this stage is made by affidavit rather than automatically given by oral evidence. An affidavit is written evidence, a concise statment of everything you wish to tell the court.

You will see that obtaining an injunction is not as simple as an ordinary judgement for payment of money.

For an injunction which is heard soon after the application, the court's main aim is to look for the balance of convenience – how it can regulate the problem so that neither party is unnecessarily prejudiced. The purpose of the hearing is not to determine the whole matter, but to come to a compromise on the issue for the time being. This normally means that the matter is in practice determined. It may involve the court insisting on the plaintiff promising compensation to the defendant if the injunction means that the defendant will be unreasonably prejudiced.

It is rather like an agreement that the parties might be able to come to themselves without the court by the making of an order.

Where there are claims on both sides, the judge will often propose that both parties promise to the court not to cause the problems that have arisen. These promises are known as undertakings and are as good as injunctions for the purposes of enforcement of the promise.

Possession proceedings against a tenant

Evicting a tenant, even after the lease has expired, generally involves obtaining an order of the court where the tenant is reluctant to move out of the property (*see* Recovering possession of the property, page 95). Failure to follow the procedure can be serious, and a tenant should never be evicted except by due process of law. This is now the case whether the tenant has a proper lease or is a mere licensee.

For occasions when court proceedings do not have to be used (apart from when the tenant is cooperative) *see* Licences, page 81.

Where court proceedings are necessary there are three choices to the landlord as to the procedure he may wish to follow to obtain a court order, depending on the type of lease:

1 Summons This is much the same as the method outlined above in relation to proceedings for money judgements, although a different form is used – the request for issue of summons for possession of land, another kind of fixed date action.

Particulars of claim have to be prepared, which the court staff may help you with, but seek the assistance of a solicitor on this point, since the court is strict as to what goes into the pleadings before it. It is essential that you state

- the address of the property
- whether it is a residential house
- details of the lease that governs the tenancy
- the grounds on which possession is claimed.

2 Accelerated possession procedure Where the tenant resides under an assured shorthold or assured tenancy, this quicker procedure may be available to the landlord. This procedure can only be used when the landlord is relying on Grounds 1 or 3 in the case of an assured tenancy. If the court is satisfied that the landlord has grounds for possession, just by looking at the application and the tenant's reply, there is no need for a hearing.

However, if the landlord needs to recover arrears of rent as well, then the fixed date summons procedure has to be used.

The tenant is also able to apply to the court to set aside the decision of the court to grant the landlord possession within 14 days of the order. The application is to be made on a special form which is available from the county court.

3 Originating application This is only appropriate when there is a Rent Act tenancy, and the landlord wishes to rely on the mandatory cases.

Possession proceedings against squatters
This form of action is made by an originating action for which there is a prescribed form (available from any legal stationers). If you have squatters it is likely that you will not know their names, but the court makes provision for this and the form can be adapted. There are special procedures which must be followed when serving the application on the squatters. You will need to complete and swear an affidavit, in which you must state:

- how you have a stake in the land, whether by ownership or by a lease
- the circumstances in which the property is now occupied by squatters
- that you do not know their names if this is the case.

If you know all their names, then service of the documents can take place in the ordinary way, and a court bailiff will take care of this matter. However, in the event of your not knowing their names, the documents need to be placed in sealed transparent envelopes addressed to 'the occupiers'. These are then fixed to the front door and posted through the letter box. It is the court's concern that the squatters will definitely know that you have issued the proceedings, so that they can exercise their right to answer your case.

Once you get judgement, you can get a warrant for possession from the court within three months. The court bailiff can help you get rid of the squatters once you have the warrant, and you can evict any squatters you find on your property, even if they are not named in the warrant or application.

Enforcing your court order

The order may still have to enforced after winning in court. If you have obtained an injunction or an undertaking and the defendant continues to act in contravention of it despite being served with the order, then he is in contempt of court – he has refused to obey the order of the judge, or has broken a promise that he made to the court.

Where the defendant is in breach of an injunction order, you may apply to have them committed to prison for contempt of court. This is a drastic action which the court will only take in the event of very flagrant breaches of the order. But it may be worth letting the defendant know that you are serious, particularly since you went to all the trouble of going to court in the first place. The appropriate form here is N78, which will need to be supported by an affidavit from you and any other witnesses. The judge will hear the matter rather like a criminal trial, but with the person aggrieved as the prosecutor, rather than the Crown Prosecution Service. A maximum sentence of two years' imprisonment can be made for contempt of court.

If the defendant has not paid money that you have been awarded, you can ask the court to enforce the judgement by any of the following methods:

1 A warrant of execution gives the bailiffs authority to visit the defendant at his home or business to either get him to pay, or take the equivalent value from his possessions to sell at auction.
2 An attachment of earnings order can be made which orders the defendant's employer to dock his wages by a certain amount each week or month that he is paid and send it to the court. The court will then send the money on to you.
3 Garnishee orders freeze the defendant's bank or building society account, and arrange for the money to be paid to you. A garnishee order can also be made against the defendant's debtors, so that they pay the money to you rather than the defendant.

The court will demand a fee for enforcing the judgement, recoverable from the defendant.
- For warrants of execution and attachment of earnings orders the rate is 15p for every pound claimed, with a minimum fee of £10 and a maximum of £80.
- Applications for a garnishee order cost £30.
- Warrants of possession cost £50 flat fee.

USEFUL ADDRESSES

Architects and Surveyors Institute
15 St Mary Street
Chippenham
Wiltshire SN15 3JN
Telephone: 01249 444505

The Consumer's Association
(Which? Personal Service)
2 Marylebone Road
London NW1 4DF
Telephone: 0171 486 5544

Council for Registered Gas Installers
(CORGI)
4 Elmwood
Chineham Business Park
Crockford Lane
Basingstoke
Hampshire RG24 8WG
Telephone: 01256 707060

Department of Environment leaflets
available from:
Department of Environment
PO Box 151
London E15 2HF
Fax: 0181 533 1618

Environmental Health Department
(contact through your local authority,
council or borough)

Justice
11–12 Bouverie Street
London EC4Y 8BS

Land Registry (England and Wales)
Plumer House
Tailyour Road
Crownhill
Plymouth PL6 5HY
Telephone: 01752 701234

Land Tribunal for England and Wales
Dunstans House
Fetter Lane
London EC4A 1BT
Telephone: 0171 404 4954

Land Tribunal for Scotland
1 Grosvenor Crescent
Edinburgh EH12 5ER
Telephone: 0131 225 7996

Law Society
113 Chancery Lane
London WC3A 1PL
Telephone: 0171 242 1222

Law Society of Scotland
26 Drumsheugh Gardens
Edinburgh EH3 7YR
Telephone: 0131 226 7411

Law Society Northern Ireland
Law Society House
98 Victoria Street
Belfast BT1 3JZ

Mailing Preference Service
Telephone: 0171 738 1625

Mediation UK
82A Gloucester Road
Bishopstone
Bristol BS7 8BN
Telephone: 0171 924 1234

National House-building Council
Buildmark House
Chiltern Avenue
Amersham
Bucks HP6 5AP
Telephone: 01494 434477

National Inspection Council for
    Electrical Installation Contracting
    (NICEIC)
Vintage House
37 Albert Embankment
London SE1 7UJ
Telephone: 0171 582 7746

Noise Abatement Society
PO Box 518
Aynsford
Kent DA4 0LL
Telephone: 01322 862789

Register of Land (Scotland)
151 London Road
Edinburgh
Telephone: 0131 659 6111

Register of Sasines (Scotland)
Middlebank House
151 London Road
Edinburgh
Telephone: 0131 659 6111

Royal Institute of British Architects
66 Portland Place
London W1N 4AD
Telephone: 0171 580 5533

Royal Institution of Chartered
Surveyors
12 Great George Street
London SW1P 3AD
Help-line: 0171 222 7000

Royal Institution of Chartered
    Surveyors Scotland
9 Manor Place
Edinburgh EH3 7DN
Telephone: 0131 225 7078

Royal Mail
Mail redirection enquiries
Freephone: 0800 444844
Credit card payment: 0345 777888

INDEX